GRANDPA, DO YOU REMEMBER THIS?

*An artist's view
Down Memory Lane*

A pictorial view of the vast changes in
Britain
between 1936 and the "Swinging Sixties"

by
Peter Drake

*The book is divided into three parts
1. Pre-war and its approach
2. The war years
3. Post-war*

Acknowledgements

*I would like to give
thanks to the
many people
who have encouraged me
to write this book and guided me with wise advice
on how to go about it. So, firstly, thank you to the grandchild
who, many years ago asked very seriously, if I remembered the Romans.*

*Secondly Jack Boteman who has written and published over sixty books in his
native Holland and gave me very helpful advice.*

*My father who left me fifty-three years of diaries and many documents in which he
noted, in miniscule writing, the happenings of each day. The weather, who was absent
from work, what time he went to the bank, the wholesale price of butter or eggs, events
concerning his children, the Kent cricket score, births, deaths and marriages. Also
during the war how many times the siren had sounded, what time he went on duty as
an Auxiliary fireman, Chapel and Sunday School meetings he attended and even the
time of going to bed after "listening in" to the BBC.*

*Pamela Haydock has kindly encouraged me, and read and corrected my text as have
several of my children. In particular my thanks to my son Philip who, in spite of his
work load, endlessly advised me when constructing computer generated pictures, also
my brother Michael who has corrected names and places I had mis-named or forgotten
then Charles Yates who has finally professionally edited the book ready for production.*

*Like most writers my greatest thanks must go to my wife. It was she who encouraged
me to take up painting again and like so many partners of writers and artists has had
to endure long hours of loneliness as this and other work slowly developed.*

My grateful thanks are due to the following for allowing me to use their material:

Trades bike p39, Messrs James & John Graham Ltd, Penrith, Cumbria, CA11 7BS
Evacuation picture p46, Woodlands Junior School, Tonbridge, Kent, TN10 4B
"Maypole Dancing" p65, Barwick-in-Elmet Maypole Trust, Leeds, LS15 4PE
School p127, Chatham House Grammar School, Ramsgate, CT11 7PS
Smithfield Market Dispute p133, Courtesy of Times Newspapers

*I have made every effort to locate everyone who has
had their photograph or printed matter
reproduced in this work, in
some cases I have
failed and
would appreciate
that information for inclusion in any future edition.*

Section symbols

Pre-war

War-time

Post-war

CONTENTS Pages 1-100

CONTENTS *Pages 101-190*

PRE-WAR

An artist's view
DOWN MEMORY LANE

INTRODUCTION

For those of you my age this is a trip down memory lane. For the young, like my grandchild whose inocent question "Do you remember the Romans?" sparked off this book it will provide many of the answers. My story covers a period of immense change starting in the 1930s. The Victorian era did not finish with the death of the old Queen in 1901. Half the population had been born in her reign. A large proportion of the people lived in Victorian houses, cooked on the same stoves, suffered the same lack of heating and sanitary facilities, had no electricity. They handled money frequently with the old Queen's head stamped on when she was a young woman. It finishes approximately in the "Swinging Sixties".

Now time is a funny thing, I am as old as the hills: I knew both my grandfathers, born respectively in 1865 and 1869. They in turn had talked with people born in the 1700's, before the battle of Waterloo or the French revolution.People whose attitudes, beliefs and values they carried with them and to some degree passed on to me. I was born before the last World War and can vividly remember many things from my childhood but often not what I went to get upstairs a few minutes earlier. I had several moments of panic the other day when I could not for the life of me remember the name of one of my grandchildren. Other old buffers tell me not to worry as they suffer the same problem. Well, if that's the case I had better write down the little bit of history I have seen before I forget everything.

This book is in three sections: (1) Pre-war, (2) The war, (3) Post-war. Let's start by looking at a view of the country as it was was in 1936, just before the war started.

for men who, often at much risk, came forward to help the constituted authority in breaking a revolutionary strike. This is the case with over 1,000 employees of

buoy 120ft. up the cliffs in a heavy sea early yesterday when their vessel went ashore on the beach two miles north of Dimlington, near Withernsea, on the East

All her essential machinery and ment, however, hav been insta tested.

The dock trials c the 200,0

Ramsgate *but typical of many British towns in 1936*

I was born in the Dame Janet ward of Ramsgate hospital. Dame Janet Stancomb Wills was a local public benefactress. She had also contributed the town's fire engine and had doubtless done other notable good works. A model of the fire engine was my favourite toy as a three year old. In the days before the State tried to control everything from birth to death a moral responsibility fell on such as she to ease the suffering of those less fortunate. Not all did so. Others who had taken an interest in the welfare of the town were Lady Rose Wygall whose home was in St Lawrence, then a village suburb of the town, and Sir Moses Montifiore who had a large house on the East Cliff. Interesting characters but from my father's time so I shall not bore you with them.

The Royal Harbour of Ramsgate in 1954

My Ramsgate was a holiday resort and had been for the previous 150 years, mainly for Londoners, it had a population of about 36,000. Basic day to day life there was much like any other town. It had a port which had never paid a profit in spite of enjoying the title Royal Harbour of Ramsgate ever since a visit by George IV in 1822. There was an extensive railway sorting yard and repair sheds, a Georgian atmosphere and a substantial summer holiday trade, much of it from London. Many residents were Welsh miners recruited to the area for the four Kent coal mines, the nearest being Chislet Colliery in Upstreet, a fifteen minute journey up the line towards Canterbury. All have now disappeared together with the hundreds of other coalmines in the UK. Very few British coal mines are still in existence, all are private. At that time it also had two airfields, Manston of WW2 fame and Pyson's Road for light aircraft were I had my first flight at a fair in about 1957.

I arrived into a very different world from that in which we now live. It was February 1936. Very few people had a car or phone. Most people wore the same clothes all week.

Saturday night was bath night to be clean for best clothes on Sunday. Films were in black and white, so were most men in their grey trousers and white shirts, admittedly some had a pinstripe but gaily coloured shirts did not arrive until I was at art college sixteen years later and even then were regarded as a trifle exotic. Baths, basins and toilets were uniformly white as were sheets, men's underpants and vests. For some curious reason those for ladies were a sort of salmon pink and their knickers, the legs of which were elasticated, reached almost to their knees. It was not an uncommon sight to see middle aged ladies groping up under their longish skirts to find their handkerchief which was safely tucked up under the elastic. Cars were almost all black and most town buildings had a black skin of soot from the coal fires and coal burning steam trains. Towns looked drab but at least old ladies walked down the street without the expectation of being mugged. People said "Good morning" to those they passed in the road. Men automatically raised their hats to women they knew. Schoolboys also raised their caps to schoolmasters as they scurried past, or got a detention for failing to do so. Men shook hands on a deal without the need of a contract to ensure the transaction would be honoured. Vast sections of the population had no bathroom or inside toilet. Few had central heating, university was for the wealthy or high achievers.

The Dame Janet fire engine and my favourite toy to show how the crew travelled. With its brass bell clanging and the firemen hanging on it was a very dramatic sight for a small boy.

Food hygiene

Except for "Bakerlite" and other compositions used for making hard moulded objects or containers or for insulation such as light switches and bulb holders, no plastics were available in the 1930s. Soft, flexible plastics were for the future so

This view illustrates the dramatic difference in the appearance of similar buildings after the soot has been removed following the ban on coal fires and with trains changing from steam to electric or diesel fuel. Britain is now a much brighter place in which to live. The Clean Air Act was passed in 1956 and revised in 1968 and 1993.

food was wrapped in greaseproof paper, paper bags, paper curled round in a cone shape for sweets or chips, or in old newspapers for fish and chips. Of course wrapping like this is regarded as dangerously unhygienic by our power crazed Health and Safety authority. I am happy to say that neither I nor anyone of my acquaintaince has suffered any ill effects from it. That authority has managed to build its self a huge empire that regards everyone else as far too stupid to look after themselves. People like myself who have wired countless houses over the years to the total satisfaction of various Electricity Boards may no longer do so even in our own kitchen unless the Ministry Inspector checks it. I await with anticipation an HM inspectorate division whose duty is to ensure that housewives are wearing insulated mittens when doing their ironing and children in baths are wearing lifebelts.

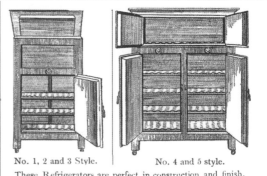

No. 1, 2 and 3 Style.   No. 4 and 5 style.

These Refrigerators are perfect in construction and finish. Cold Dry Air is always circulating, and all kinds of Perishable Viands can be kept in splendid condition during the Hottest Weather.

No Odours and no Dampness.

Uses Less Ice and keeps Colder than any other Refrigerator.

Pre-war, few could afford this domestic luxury. Anyway, these refrigerators had no power supply, just ice, but I remember seeing a shop with one operated by gas and being amazed that heat could make things cold.

Fishmongers and butchers bought ice in large blocks from an ice company who, in my town, maintained a cellar deep in the chalk along Dumpton Park Drive on Ramsgate's East Cliff. Refrigerated cabinets were not available. Shops for butchers, fishmongers and greengrocers had shutters but frequently no glass windows. Meat, fish and poultry were open to the street, often hung from hooks outside their shop or laid on a slab but I believe

Strictly speaking this picture should not be included as Mr Thomas, whose shop stood near Chatham Street in Boundary Road, sold out a short while before I was born. He had been our family's butcher since the beginning of the century and this photo illustrates the situation at that time. Long queues formed on Saturday mornings to ensure the freshest possible meat for Sunday.

the population survived because they had from birth been exposed to little doses of infection and developed immunity to those commonly contracted. Long after the war it was not unusual to see a butcher's doorway blocked by the carcass of a pig strung up by the hind legs to hooks set into the lintel while the butcher split it from top to bottom. When we lived in Lamberhurst during the war a cat frequently slept in the shop window of the local baker. Nobody passed away from Cat disease to my knowledge. Whether there are fewer cases of food poisoning with all the new legislation I do not know but suspect people now lack the antibody protection my generation built up through childhood contact with more germs. Children in under developed countries survive in conditions that would kill us. So some contact with germs can apparently protect us.

Law and order

Without coke cans, plastic bottles and wrapping the world was also much tidier, aided I suspect, by the much greater respect and, or fear of children for adults. Throwing down rubbish in the street was likely to cause one the embarrassment of being told to pick it up and put it in the bin. We did not answer back for fear of a clout. Fear is a necessary ingredient in society. A baby's hand can be held near a teapot while the parent says "hot", teaching the child the fear of burning. It remembers it for ever. Fear of fines and losing points on driving licences does wonders for calming traffic. I suggest that fear of authority could result in much better behaviour among the young of today. It is not that we were better children, it was just because an adult had no fear if he or she corrected a child. A policeman could give you a cuff on the ear or the Park Keeper a whack with his stick if he caught you up to mischief. We did not bleat about these things because if we complained to our parents they would likely repeat the punishment for letting down the family. Government is now trying to force discipline by taking all correctional powers to themselves and are amazed at their failure without, for a moment, considering how much cheaper and more efficient it would be to allow citizens to continue a system that has worked much more efficiently for hundreds of years. It wasn't perfect and never will be, there were abuses power but it worked much better than the current one. If you don't believe me look at the age group that now commits the majority of hooligan crime in the UK, then compare it with the pre-war figures.

The 1940's local policeman, on foot or his bike, knew the people in his area and we knew him. In many cases he was in one place for years. He could warn people if their behaviour was unacceptable without resorting to heavy handed Court action. While living in a village I recall when a smallholder called the police because school

The uniform and equipment of the police has changed dramatically. The constable pictured here would have at his command a whistle, torch, pencil or pen, notebook and in a long pocket in his trouser leg, a truncheon. This perhaps gave rise to the joke comparison between English and American police: the American draws his gun and calls out "Stop or I'll shoot." The English bobby blows his whistle and shouts "Stop or I'll shout Stop again." There were no flak jackets, radios or the guns that we now see as necessary for many policemen and women. Armed robbery was rare.

13

children had been throwing pebbles at his ducks. The copper reminded him of an occasion many years before when he, as a child, had committed the same stupidity and asked him not to make a great affair out of it. He then went to the parents of the offenders and made it clear to each that the offence was not to be repeated.

Maybe part of our problem nowadays is that we all have cars so that passing one another in the street, on foot, occurs much less frequently giving us less contact with those around us, therefore less of a social conscience or sense of responsibility to our neighbours or neighbourhood. In the past young adults married in their 20's and most frequently settled close to their parents. Comparatively full employment meant there was no need to move far away to get work, consequently young people knew, or at least recognised, most of those they passed in the street.

The police patrol car of the 30's and 40's was the black MG.

Salaries and house prices

Throughout the reign of Queen Victoria an ordinary working man was paid about one pound per week. That stability was disrupted by WW1 and then the years of depression. The following advertisements from the Times news paper published on the day of my birth gives a fair idea of wage levels in 1936.

MARRIED Couple, Cook and Indoor Manservant, wanted; family three; £120; sitting room with wireless; gas cooker; state ages.—Mrs. Stirling, care of British Agency, London Road, Horsham. Tele. 774. No fees. (Also Female Servants' Registry.)

SINGLE gentleman requires Married Couple as Cook and Parlourman; complete charge; comfortable post; £104; state ages.—L. Brady, Esq., care of British Agency, London Road, Horsham. Tele. 774. No fees. (Also Female Servants' Registry.)

HOUSE-PARLOURMAN required immediately, accus-

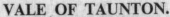

VALE OF TAUNTON.

BUTLER, 37; £90; excellent personal reference.—Abbey's Agency, 37, Berners Street, W.1. Museum 1373, 6053.

DOWER HOUSE.

£1 Per Week.—Young Man, about 16; office, motor engineers.—Beardmore, 26, Queen's Road, W.2.

16 ACRES AND COTTAGE. £2,250.

GLOS. 400 FEET UP. LOVELY VIEWS.
  Dating from 1730. In first-rate order. Panelling old oak. Lounge hall, 3 reception, 8-9 bed and dressing (several with basins h. and c.), 2 bath rooms; Co.'s electric light; stabling, garage; fascinating Gardens, hard tennis court, pasture, woodlands and orchard. FREEHOLD. Inspected by WELLESLEY-SMITH and Co., 91-93, Baker Street, London, W.1. Tele., Welbeck 4583.

FASCINATING 16TH CENTURY

RESIDENCE. COMPLETELY MODERNIZED.

  SOMERSET.—Panelled lounge hall, 3 reception, 8 bed rooms, 2 bath rooms; old oak beams and open fireplaces; Co.'s electric light and water; splendid outbuildings; loose boxes; cottage; old-world gardens and orchards. Freehold.

4 ACRES. £2,500.

FOR management of café and four shops, Birmingham area, a Manager or responsible lady Manageress; must have had thorough training in café and kitchen work and retail shop work. Position involves buying and office work and general supervision of staff of about 50. Would suit an energetic, well-educated, and refined lady with experience and flair or an experienced and able manager. Remuneration according to ability; minimum £300 p.a.—Write Box M.597, The Times, E.C.4.

Wages for domestic staff were per annum. Many had to live in so board and lodging were supplied but they were always on call.

Telephones

Even the youngest child now expects to have a mobile phone which will take photos, videos, sound alarms, tell the time, connect it to the internet and let it continue chattering to the friend in whose company he or she has just spent the day. Verbal diarrhoea has hit the world in an unprecedented way. On train journeys, or in cafes, we are obliged to listen to the most detailed incidents in the lives of people in whom we have no interest.

A black daffodil

In those far off days phones were used for emergencies, to order goods or to enquire the health of someone. I doubt if a phone call ever lasted ten minutes except between couples seriously in love. Earlier phones had been a box on the wall with a handle one wound vigorously to call an operator. Next, phones resembled, and were often referred to as black daffodils, later units had a dial for calling local numbers. For other calls one dialled 'o' and asked the operator to make the connection. Nowadays sophisticated electronics allow one wire to carry multiple calls simultaneously. Then, each phone had to have its own wire connection right back to the exchange where the operators pulled out plugs on their switch board and put them into new holes to complete the circuit to the customer's correspondent. Phones were few until after the war; in a population of around 36,000 our number was Ramsgate 169. Operators sometimes illegally listened to conversations; sometimes quite usefully. Trying to contact someone, the operator might say "Oh it's no good calling at the moment he has an appointment at the doctor's now", or knowing the habits of their customers, "I should try again in half an hour, I've just seen him on the way to the bank". As demand increased phone numbers became longer using letters as well as numbers. In London to call the Richmond area one dialled RIC and then the number or BAT for Battersea. Mobile phones have re-introduced letters on the dial to facilitate text messaging. Next came national dialling followed by international dialling. Each time businesses had to reprint all their notepaper etc. with the latest digits. Red public phone boxes were used by most people and a local call cost 2pence for three minutes in the 30s and 40s.

To correspond urgently with someone who had no telephone. The Post Office had a telegraph service. For six old pence one could send a message of not more than nine words, plus a ha'penny for each extra word, by filling in a telegram form at the Post Office. The message was transmitted by phone to the recipient's nearest post office then delivered by a lad in a smart navy blue uniform, on a bike. Telegrams tended to be received with trepidation because, being comparatively expensive, were only used in emergency and frequently bore bad news. During the wartime they were particularly dreaded, "We regret to tell you your son/husband has been killed in action."

My aunt was trapped in India for the entire war. When it finished my parents booked a phone call to her for Christmas. First a letter had to be sent to warn her to be at a phone to receive it and supply its number. It travelled by ship, there were no inter-continental flights to India. It had to be sent about three months in advance to allow time for a reply. Next the call had to be booked. This entailed all the operators in each country ensuring an unbroken wire connection between England and her part of India while observing the time difference in each country. What an achievement. We were allowed to talk for five minutes. Now, sitting on a park bench in Essex, I can check what is happening on the news, or call a goat herder in Mongolia and transmit a live video of my surroundings.

A 1936 office manual switchboard

Medicine and surgery

The King James bible of 1611 AD tells us that "The dayes of our yeres are threescore yeeres and ten" i.e. seventy. When I started work in 1953 the aver-age lifespan of a man was down to sixty-six, only one year into retire-ment. Fortunately, by steady steps, we now see a hundred as a common possi-bility. All medical treatment was private. Basically doctors charged wealthy people a lot and much less to those who were not. 1948 saw the introduction of the National Health Service. Doctors were at the top of the ladder along with hospital matrons, fearsome dragons who ruled with a rod of iron and ensured the smooth running of their empire. There now seems to be an army of admin-istrators at various levels, but a desperate shortage of beds, well qualified doctors and nursing staff, however our survival chances are much greater.

During my travels I have found that in many countries there is no need to consult a doctor then wait months for a specialist appointment while the problem gets worse. For instance, suffer a chest pain, go to a cardiologist. If he says it is probably indigestion not a heart problem, he instantly refers the patient to an appropriate consultant who may, after examination, decide the malady is something that can be adequately sorted by a general practitioner. If urgent, one gets seen the same day. Need an MRI scan? You are given a prescription and you go your local scan clinic. The result is in your own sticky fingers usually within the week, frequently the same day. X-rays and ECGs are in your hand before leaving the department and you personally transport them back to the specialist. Fast scans and diagnoses result in early treatment. Result: less stress or time in hospital, faster turnover of bed space. More money for equipment. Nobody is more interested than you in seeing that the right person receives your X-ray, scan or report than you; all are ready within hours, surely patients can be trusted to cart them to the specialist instead of having them lie endlessly in an administrator's tray. Patients frequently wait and worry themselves silly for a few weeks, or months, or sadly but not uncommonly, die before this elevated man can fit them in. Twice I have been hospitalised on a Friday with no appropriate specialist available till Monday. True there was a specialist on duty but I was not in his field of specialisation. Why? Catch problems early. Imagine its Friday, your car coughs, and dies half way home in the rain. The AA say "Sorry chum, our specialist mechanic will be with you on Monday with luck but you know, we get quite a backlog over the weekend". Why should we be satisfied with less with our lives at stake?

During my early years I caught all the normal illnesses, chickenpox, measles, German measles and mumps needing the services of our local medic, aptly named Dr Stitch. A gruff person, but I believe a very caring man. Doctors of that era were treated very respectfully no matter whether they were gruff, jovial, or downright uncaring. People of my parents' generation did not dream of questioning their doctor's judgement. Internet information now allows us to query the doctor's diagnosis or dicuss alternative treatments. Scarlet fever, now very rare, was treated in an Isolation Hospital, all toys and clothes accompanying the patient were burnt.

16

In 1929 this country suffered about 34,000 deaths from diptheria. As a baby I had been inoculated against smallpox, and in 1941 against diptheria as mass inoculations against it started that year. By 1950 diptheria had been almost eradicated. You can now be protected from a wide range of problems, German measles, poliomyelitis, flu, meningitis, whooping cough, and tetanus. A few years later there were many additional protections available for a range of illnesses found in other parts of the world.

In 1936 many people, young and old, still died from what are now regarded as comparatively minor ailments. Just a few days of raspberry or banana flavoured antibiotics and all is now well. At that time if one developed a temperature you were swaddled up in bed to sweat out the fever, dosed with Aspirin and your forehead sponged with cold water. If that failed you died. Mass production of the first antibiotic, Penicillin, started in 1948 and transformed the situation. Early versions of antibiotics attacked germs willy nilly. The disadvantage being that if the next illness to hit you was treated with the same antibiotic, it was less likely to be successful, particularly if the first course had not been properly completed. It may also be that the manufacturing of early products resulted in a less pure item than nowadays. Today the range of antibiotics is vast and they are increasingly specific to a particular problem, attacking a particular type of infection, not lashing out at every target.

My Grandma Cain was born in 1874. On her 100th birthday I asked her if she regretted the passing of the old ways; she had, after all, more experience than most of the changing world so was well qualified to pass an opinion. She appeared to drop off to sleep for a short while as one is entitled to at that age, then suddenly opened her eyes and said "I had all my teeth out without anaesthetic." I think that was a pretty good answer though it is strange as laughing gas (nitrous oxide) was already largely used by dentists during her youth. She had lived in a small village so perhaps the local man was incapable of using it. She did not bother to mention she had also had both breasts removed, one in 1914 and the other in 1917, with laughing gas, chloroform or ether as the anaesthetic. These act fast but stop acting fast when the supply terminates. Now surgeons have cocktails of anaesthetics to choose from so that the patient's pain can be softened over a period of time instead of going from unconsciousness to agony immediately after an operation. It is easy in these days of keyhole surgery, to forget that not long ago the aftershock of intrusive surgery often killed, or patients needed an extensive recovery period and a stay in a convalescent home before they could safely be released.

My youngest brother, David, was born in 1946 with a heart defect. What was termed a blue baby because of the blueish tinge poor circulation gave the skin. Doctors at the time of his birth told my parents that he was unlikely to live beyond the age of five. In fact he died just before his 20th birthday, two years before the South African surgeon, Dr Barnard, did his first heart transplant. Had he been born thirty years later he would probably have had surgery within a few months of his birth and lived a perfectly normal life.

The week

In many ways 1930's life was a much less complicated than now but entailed a lot of drudgery especially for women. A woman's week started on Monday with cooking breakfast. She then faced the first three days of the week occupied with washing, rinsing, wringing, drying and ironing. Evenings were for darning socks and other clothing repairs or knitting. This was relieved each Sunday with church attendance by much of the population. At that time there were fourteen churches in my town to serve a population of 36,000. Many now converted to shops or warehouses. Our working week went Monday to Saturday lunchtime. Pre-war families tended to eat considerably more meat than most people do today provided they could afford it. Saturday afternoon was shopping or sport, usually watching football at the local football field followed by bath night. Those in very dirty jobs often showered at work. Sunday was Church and best clothes followed by roast lunch. Monday, clean clothes from last weeks wash. For the women, laundry and leftover roast for dinner. Tuesday the rest of the Sunday roast minced as shepherd's pie, rissoles or bubble and squeak, Wednesday stew, Thursday, liver or kidneys, Friday fish. Saturday was usually something cold. Talking to others of my generation I find this was fairly standard. Many years later I asked my mother if we and/or people in general were smelly as a result of the lack of showers or baths and the same clothes being worn all the working week? She said she supposed so but had never noticed it at the time. Those without a bathing facility or hot water where they lived could use the Public Baths available in the towns.

On Sundays all shops were closed by a law enforced by the Lord's Day Observance Society.

Monday morning was when all Britian did its washing.

My earliest memory is of a woman looking under the green lined, cream tasselled sunshade into my pram. I must have recognised her as I foresaw that she was going to poke her finger under my chin, presumably because it produced a reaction in other babies more favourable to being poked about, I just wished she would go away. I must have been between one-and-a-half and two years old as after that it would have been my brother in the pram. He arrived in April after my second birthday. Another early memory is of crawling round the living room and looking up at the underside of the bay window sill. Why wasn't it painted? Just because grownups didn't look at it? Later, as a building contractor I always took care to ensure the undersides were painted though I doubt if anyone over three-years old ever noticed.

Summer 1939

Life for us children continued as normal during the summer of 1939. My cousins, Eileen and Margaret, and their parents came to stay with their grandparents who had a drapery shop in Grange Road. Saturday afternoons were frequently spent on the beach at the western undercliff sailing a little wooden yacht in the paddling pool. I suppose this was the start of my fascination with sailing.

I recall Eileen being knocked over by a wave slightly larger than the rest and her grandfather, my Great Uncle Bert, rushing into the sea to drag her out of the undertow and getting the bottoms of his trousers wet. I also remember being astonished that he then felt it necessary to return home to dry out his trouser legs. Why would anyone want to leave a lovely beach for such a paltry reason. To my surprise he didn't come back that afternoon. Now I am a great grandfather myself and can understand that the event provided him with a sound reason to escape screaming children and have his afternoon nap before we all returned for tea.

Teatime was an institution in Britain, a light meal that has more or less disappeared from our daily life. The men being at work except during holidays or weekend afternoons, this was largely a woman's thing. A cup of tea and a sandwich between lunch and dinner or supper depending on the individual family's custom, but a genteel affair when shared with afternoon visitors. It was a chance to show off the family china and silverware

Teapot, sugar basin, milk jug and often a matching slop basin.

set out on the best tablecloth, frequently hand embroidered as part of the woman's trousseau, made before her marriage and stored in her bottom drawer against that day. At my great aunt's house it was invariably at 4.30, prepared before parting for the afternoon's activities.

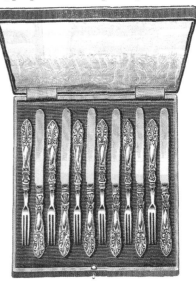

In consequence my great-aunt's Shipham's fish or meat paste sandwiches and those filled with mustard and cress took on the look more recently associated with British Rail offerings. The top slice forming a happy, if dried out, smile while the lower one was inclined to hug onto the plate.

Cake stands which were lined with a white paper doyly.

Set of tea knives and forks.

She was also a dab hand at a rather desiccated sponge cake. With rationing this was restricted to one slice and only after eating several sandwiches.

19

The Air Display

This air display was the subject of dispute between my father and I some forty years later. I claimed to clearly remember being taken to an air display at nearby Manston aerodrome. "Rubbish" said he, "You must have dreamed it." Now my father was a diary keeper, an ardent, lifetime diary keeper. I have fifty three years of his diaries detailing the daily weather, what he did in the morning, the afternoon, the evening. What time he went to the bank. Which employee was starting, leaving, or on holiday and also noted any important news event. All this in a microscopic scrawl that could cause blindness if studied intensively. I once criticised it in his office. He claimed his secretary had no difficulty in reading it, but when I referred to her she admitted that she often had to consult others and typed whatever was the consensus opinion leaving him to correct errors when he came to sign his correspondence. Some weeks later he rang to say he had checked his diary and confirmed that I was quite correct and the display had been held on 28 May 1938, when I was aged two years and three months.

My vivid recollection is of worrying that the pilot of a biplane had got in his machine, but perhaps not shut the cockpit door properly and was in imminent danger of falling to his death. Actually it has no door. I failed to understand that catastrophe was averted by the pilot's harness which the shoulder high cockpit hid from my view. I also saw a tri-plane, three parallel wings, which I had never seen before nor since. Such early aircraft, and even biplanes, were shortly superseded by the much faster and safer mono-planes with enclosed cockpits and retractable wheels. The Spitfire was on the horizon. However many missions were flown by biplanes during WW2, their only advantage being that some shellfire passed through their fabric covered wings without impeding the aircraft as they passed at about 110 mph. Remember that flying was still only thirty years old. In the next few years it was to take gigantic steps forwards due to the war.

During the Battle of Britain I stood with my father in mid Kent and watched the spiralling vapour trails of the Spitfires and Hurricanes, like woolly spaghetti, as they fought for supremacy nearer the coast.

By curious coincidence I was also at the following Manston air display held at on 18th September 1948. During a flying demonstration a Mosquito light bomber did a victory roll but went out of control. One wing seemed to get ahead of the other and it just tumbled over and over, fluttering down like a falling leaf and landing several miles away taking the top deck off a double-decker bus with a considerable loss of life.

*The price of 67/6
equals £3.38p now*

Flying was a cold business in an open cockpit. Aircrew flying closed fighters and bombers were obliged to sit in one position for many hours at a time with no heating and in the case of bombers, flying at high, sub zero altitudes to avoid enemy guns it was also exceedingly cold.

CIVIL DEFENCE

YOUR FOOD IN WAR-TIME

PUBLIC INFORMATION LEAFLET NO. 4

Read this and keep it carefully.

You may need it.

Issued from the Lord Privy Seal's Office July, 1939

Threat of war

By 1938 the warnings of Winston Churchill were being taken seriously. Britain was re-arming. It was becoming clear that Germany was well advanced with rebuilding its army and constructing the implements of war in defiance of the agreement made at the end of the Great War of 1914-1918. Hitler annexed Austria and silenced all opposition. The British Prime Minister, Mr Chamberlain, attended the Munich Conference and was assured of "Peace in our Time" by Hitler who then invaded Czechoslovakia. Fearing the worse, the Government issued this warning leaflet to the population and set out plans to distribute supplies in the event of an invasion of our shores.

YOUR FOOD IN WAR-TIME

You know that our country is dependent to a very large extent on supplies of food from overseas. More than 20 million tons are brought into our ports from all parts of the world in the course of a year. Our defence plans must therefore provide for the protection of our trade routes by which these supplies reach us, for reserves of food here and for the fair distribution of supplies, both home and imported, as they become available.

WHAT THE GOVERNMENT HAVE DONE

During the last eighteen months the Government have purchased considerable reserves of essential foodstuffs which are additional to the commercial stocks normally carried. This is one of the precautionary measures which has been taken to build up our resources to meet the conditions of war. In addition, the necessary arrangements have been made to control the supply and distribution of food throughout the country immediately upon the outbreak of hostilities and to bring in such measure of rationing as may be required.

HOW YOU CAN HELP

There are certain ways in which traders and householders can help to strengthen our food position at the present time.

In the ordinary way, the stocks of food in any area are based on the extent of the local demand, or the size of the local population. In war time, the amount of stocks in any area might be affected by air raid damage, or the flow of supplies might be reduced temporarily by transport difficulties.

As an additional precaution against difficulties of this kind, traders will be doing a good service *now* by maintaining, and if possible increasing, their stocks, so far as they can. You, too, as an ordinary householder, will be doing a good service if you can manage to get in some extra stores of food that will keep. These will be a stand-by against an emergency. Of course, there are many of us who cannot do this, but those who can will find, if a strain is put at any time upon local supplies, that such reserves will not only be a convenience to themselves but will help their neighbours. By drawing on these reserves instead of making demands on the shops at such a time, they would leave the stocks available for the use of those who have not been able to put anything by.

For those who have the means, a suitable amount of foodstuffs to lay by would be the quantity that they ordinarily use in one week. The following are suggested as articles of food suitable for householder's storage:—

Meat and fish in cans or glass jars; flour; suet; canned or dried milk; sugar; tea; cocoa; plain biscuits.

When you have laid in your store, you should draw on it regularly for day to day use, replacing what you use by new purchases, so that the stock in your cupboard is constantly being changed. Flour and suet in particular should be replaced frequently. You may find it helpful to label the articles with the date of purchase.

Any such reserves should be bought before an emergency arises. To try to buy extra quantities when an emergency is upon us, would be unfair to others.

FOOD SUPPLIES FOR EVACUATION

The Government evacuation scheme, of which you have already been told, will mean a considerable shift of population from the more vulnerable areas to safer areas. This will lead to additional demands on shops in the reception areas. Traders have been asked to have plans in readiness for increasing the supplies in shops in reception areas to meet the needs of the increased population. It would, however, take a day or two for these plans to be put into full operation.

The Government are, therefore, providing emergency supplies for children and others travelling under the official evacuation scheme. These supplies would be issued to them on their arrival in their new areas and would be sufficient for two days. Those who receive them will be asked not to make any purchases, other than small ones, in the local shops during those two days.

Those making their own arrangements to travel, should take food with them sufficient for two days, and should buy in advance, as part of their arrangements, the non-perishable food which they would require. As already said, anyone who, in time of emergency, buys more than normal quantities, would be doing harm, as such buying must draw on stocks which should be available for others.

NATIONAL HOUSEKEEPING IN WAR TIME

CENTRAL CONTROL

Should war come, the Government would take over responsibility for obtaining the main food supplies for the country, and for distributing them through all the stages down to the consumer. This would ensure that every precaution could be taken against war time risks. The prices of food would be controlled and supplies directed wherever they were needed.

For this purpose, the existing organisation of the food trades would be used so far as possible, and all food traders—importers, manufacturers, wholesalers and retailers—would work under the direction of a Ministry of Food. The Ministry would act for the benefit of the country as a whole and be assisted by representatives of the various trades.

LOCAL DISTRIBUTION

In each area food control would be in the hands of a local committee, which would be set up at the outbreak of war. The membership of these committees would be chosen to represent the general body of consumers in the area. It would include a few retail traders who possess a first-hand working knowledge of trading conditions.

The principal duty of these local Food Control Committees would be to look after the interests of consumers. They will also be responsible for supervising retail distribution. Shopkeepers would be licensed to trade by these committees. Ordinarily, all

This leaflet was issued in July 1939 and other reports state that gas masks were issued prior to the start of the war; however, we were issued ours well after our evacuation to Lamberhurst in June 1940.

Later, additional advice for windows was to stick gummed brown paper tape diagonally across the panes in the form of a St Andrew's cross to minimise injuries from flying glass in the event of bomb blast. I remember reading that thousands of tons of shattered glass travelling at supersonic speed shredded all in its path after the Hiroshima atom bomb was dropped.

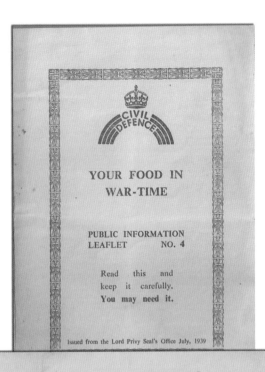

CIVIL DEFENCE

YOUR FOOD IN WAR-TIME

PUBLIC INFORMATION
LEAFLET NO. 4

Read this and
keep it carefully.
You may need it.

Issued from the Lord Privy Seal's Office July, 1939

YOUR GAS MASK

TAKE CARE OF YOUR GAS MASK AND YOUR GAS MASK WILL TAKE CARE OF YOU. It is possible that in war your life might depend on your gas mask and the condition in which it had been kept.

The official gas mask, or respirator, consists of a metal container filled with material which absorbs the gas, and a rubber facepiece with a non-inflammable transparent window. Some people seem to think that this mask does not look as if it would offer very good protection. Actually, it has been most carefully designed and fully tested, and will give you adequate protection against breathing any of the known war gases. But remember it will not protect you from the ordinary gas that you burn in a gas cooker or gas fire.

HOW TO STORE IT

Your mask should be kept carefully. Never hang it up by the straps which fasten it on over the head. This will pull the rubber facepiece out of shape so that it no longer fits you properly. It should be kept in the special box provided, where this has been issued, but any box which is air tight, or nearly so, will do.

When placed in the box the metal container should lie flat with the rubber facepiece uppermost, the transparent window lying evenly on top at full length. Great care should be taken not to bend or fold the window, or to let it get scratched, cracked or dented.

Keep the box in a cool place away from strong light. Exposure to heat or prolonged exposure to strong light will spoil the material of the mask and it may cease to give complete protection. It should never be held close to a fire or hot water pipes, or left lying out in the sun.

HOW TO PUT IT ON AND TAKE IT OFF

It is important to know how to put on your mask quickly and properly. You might need to do this in a hurry. To put it on, hold the mask by each of the side straps with the thumbs underneath and the inside of the window facing you. Then lift the mask to your face, push your chin forwards into it and draw the straps over the top of your head as far as they will go. See that the straps are properly adjusted and leave them so.

To remove the mask, insert the thumb under the buckle at the back of your head and then pull it forward over the top of your head so that the mask is lowered downwards from the face.

NEVER TRY TO LIFT THE MASK OFF UPWARDS OR BY PULLING THE CONTAINER OR THE EDGE OF THE RUBBER AT THE CHIN.

To prevent the window from misting over when the mask is worn, wet the end of a finger and rub it on a piece of toilet soap. Then rub the finger all over the inside of the window so as to leave a thin film of soap.

PUTTING YOUR MASK AWAY

After the mask has been used you will find that it is wet on the inside with moisture from the breath. This should be wiped off with a soft dry cloth and the mask allowed to dry before it is put away in its box. Do not try to dry it by applying heat.

The contents of the container do not deteriorate either with age or with wearing the mask when gas is not present. But if you suspect any flaw in your gas mask you should inform your local air raid warden.

It is a good thing to get out your gas mask occasionally and put it on, so as to get used to wearing it, and if you take the simple precautions set out above you will ensure that it is always ready for your protection.

MASKING YOUR WINDOWS

In war, one of our great protections against the dangers of air attack after nightfall would be the "black-out." On the outbreak of hostilities all external lights and street lighting would be totally extinguished so as to give hostile aircraft no indication as to their whereabouts. But this will not be fully effective unless you do your part, and see to it that no lighting in the house where you live is visible from the outside. The motto for safety will be "Keep it dark!"

Every occupier of rooms, house or flat would be responsible for darkening his own lights. Lights in the halls or on the staircases of blocks of flats or dwellings would be the responsibility of the landlord or owner.

Of course, the most convenient way of shutting in the light is to use close fitting blinds. These can be of any thick, dark coloured material such as dark blue or black or dark green glazed Holland, Lancaster or Italian Cloth.

If you cannot manage this, you could obscure your windows by fixing up sheets of black paper or thick dark brown paper mounted on battens.

Preparations for War

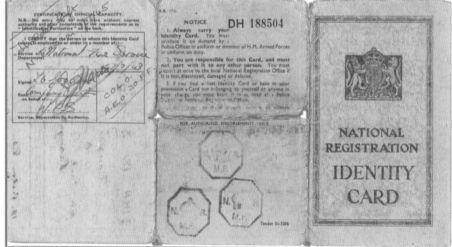

The Identity Cards of my father and self.
No photographic identification was
required and the cards were not used after
the war finished.

WAR

War declared

I remember war being announced. I was at my (Cain) grandparent's house in Sandwich. In these days of instant televised news from any part of the world it is hard to imagine radio reception of that era. The radio set, then a comparatively modern wonder, was a collection of various sized light bulbs called valves in a wooden case. About 20 inches high and 15 inches wide by 10 deep, it emitted a multitude of squeaks, whistles, hisses and shrieks until tuned exactly to the station when the often crackly voice of the BBC announcer could be heard. World news could be days out of date before it reached England as both telephone and radio communication were poor.

Because of the variable quality of reception we had to remain very quiet for my grandfather to hear the news. Everyone looked serious as they grouped round the radio trying to hear the Prime Minister's announcement against the background noises. I was three and a half and of course did not understand the significance of the news but I have a clear picture in my mind of the worried looks on the faces of my parents and grandparents huddled very close to the radio straining to hear and being "shushed" by my mother. I have just checked my father's diary for that day, Sunday 3 September 1939. He wrote: "We went to Sandwich arriving at 10.30 and heard Mr Neville Chamberlain's speech at 11.15 a.m." I seem to remember spending the afternoon murdering ants on the red tiles outside the patio door. My father was already in the Auxiliary Fire Service (AFS) as a part-time fireman. He had to return to duty that night. The first air raid siren of the war went off at 2.45 a.m. the following morning waking him and his fellows who had been sleeping at their station on a billiard table or the floor. It was a false alarm. The AFS had been formed to supplement the National Fire Service.

What you should know about
INVASION DANGER

You will shortly receive a leaflet "Beating the Invader," issued to all householders in the country, telling you what to do should invasion come. If invasion finds you in this town, and you are not ordered to leave, you must act on the instructions to stand firm. But you can help to defeat the invader by leaving now if you can be spared and have somewhere to go.

THIS APPLIES PARTICULARLY TO—
SCHOOL CHILDREN
MOTHERS WITH YOUNG CHILDREN
AGED AND INFIRM PERSONS
PERSONS LIVING ON PENSIONS
PERSONS WITHOUT OCCUPATION OR
LIVING IN RETIREMENT

If you are one of these, you should arrange to go to some other part of the country. You should not go to the coastal area of East Anglia (including Essex), Kent or Sussex.
School children can be registered to join school parties in the reception areas, and billets will be found for them.
If you are in need of help you can have your railway fare paid and a billeting allowance paid to any relative or friend with whom you stay. If you are going, go quickly.

TAKE YOUR—
National Registration Identity Card.
Ration Book.
Gas Mask.
Also any bank book, pensions payment order book, insurance cards, unemployment book, military registration documents, passport, insurance policies, securities, and any ready money.

[CONTINUED OVERLEAF

Preparations for invasion

With the collapse of all resistance in Belgium and France it was expected that the Germans would next attempt an invasion somewhere along the southeast coast of England; the first invasion of the country since William the Conqueror in 1066. For any who view war as an exciting experience read the instructions on this pamphlet and imagine the consequences if it involved you.

Orders for the population in SE England.

Already many of the men were in the Forces. Men and women involved in essential war work would be unable to accompany their relations to towns further from what was expected to become a war zone. Had we been invaded society would have been greatly fragmented. Posessions left in empty houses for the enemy or thieves. My elderly aunt and uncle left their furniture behind when they moved to their daughter's home in Maidstone. When they returned the whole house was empty.... but not because of the Germans.

if your house will be left unoccupied, turn off gas, electricity and water supplies and make provision for animals and birds. Lock your house securely. Blinds should be left up, and if there is a telephone line, ask the telephone exchange to disconnect it. Go to the Post Office and fill up a Redirection Notice so that they can forward your letters.

If you go and your house is unoccupied, your liability to pay rent, rates, mortgage charges, or charges under hire purchase agreements will be postponed.

It makes no difference if you leave your furniture in the house.

Private car and motor cycle owners who have not licensed their vehicles and have no petrol coupons may be allowed to use their cars or motor cycles unlicensed for one journey only and may apply to the Police for petrol coupons to enable them to secure sufficient petrol to journey to their destination.

If any of these matters are not clear, you will get further information at the local Council Offices.

ESSENTIAL WORKERS MUST STAY, particularly the following classes—

THE HOME GUARD. OBSERVER CORPS.
COASTGUARDS, COAST WATCHERS AND LIFEBOAT CREWS.
POLICE AND SPECIAL CONSTABULARY.
FIRE BRIGADE AND AUXILIARY FIRE SERVICE.
A.R.P. AND CASUALTY SERVICES.
MEMBERS OF LOCAL AUTHORITIES AND THEIR OFFICIALS AND EMPLOYEES.
WORKERS ON THE LAND.
PERSONS ENGAGED ON WAR WORK, AND OTHER ESSENTIAL SERVICES.
PERSONS EMPLOYED BY CONTRACTORS ON DEFENCE WORK.
EMPLOYEES OF WATER, SEWERAGE, GAS AND ELECTRICITY UNDERTAKINGS.
PERSONS ENGAGED IN THE SUPPLY AND DISTRIBUTION OF FOOD.
WORKERS ON EXPORT TRADES.
DOCTORS, NURSES AND CHEMISTS.
MINISTERS OF RELIGION.
GOVERNMENT EMPLOYEES.
EMPLOYEES OF BANKS.
EMPLOYEES OF TRANSPORT UNDERTAKINGS, NAMELY RAILWAYS, DOCKS, CANALS, FERRIES, AND ROAD TRANSPORT (BOTH PASSENGER AND GOODS).

When invasion is upon us it may be necessary to evacuate the remaining population of this and certain other towns. Evacuation would then be compulsory at short notice, in crowded trains, with scanty luggage, to destinations chosen by the Government. If you are not among the essential workers mentioned above it is better to go now while the going is good.

A. C. GEDDES,
REGIONAL COMMISSIONER
No. 12 (South-Eastern) Region.

March, 1941.

(13924) Wt. 47988/P1045 250,400. 2/41 K.H.K. Gp. 8

In fact the war got off to a slow start which was just as well as everyone had to be issued with an identity card to be carried at all times. The coast had to be defended in case of invasion. No more beach afternoons. A double line of scaf-

Top: An MTB.   Below: MGB's on patrol.

folding was erected all along the southern beaches where it was supposed the Germans might attempt a landing. The space between them filled with coils of barbed wire. Shallow water where low tides receded a considerable distance such as our nearby Pegwell Bay had large wooden stakes driven into it to deter seaplanes wishing to land there. The surrounding marshland and fields around Sandwich Bay were seeded with mines and on our walks towards the bay when visiting my Sandwich grandparents we saw notices saying "Warning! Mines".

I recall hearing that the son of a local landowner of much of the bay area, disregarded these notices and took a short cut across his land and was blown up as a result.   The bay road had massive concrete anti-tank blocks set across it. Numerous thick walled pill box gun emplacements were built in strategic positions to slow any enemy advance. So called because of their multisided form similar to the shape of pill boxes distributed by chemists. There are still a number of these buildings left as reminders of that period of threat to our country. All road signs in the south of the country were removed to hinder an advancing enemy. It also did a good job of confusing the natives. Road signs were cast iron, sighted on road junctions, painted white with a finger pointing in each direction to the nearest town and its distance. It is nice to see that many have been reinstated in the country lanes. Much more attractive and discreet to my eyes than the modern large variety but one has to slow down to read the black lettering which is quite small. There were no road numbers and the paint did not show up fluorescent in the dark as it does nowadays.

Barriers were erected along the cliff top to prevent people looking down on docks and harbours. Ramsgate became a base for motor torpedo and motor gun boats known respectively as MTBs and MGBs. They were very lightly built of overlapping diagonal ply; fast, powerfully armed and designed to carry out rapid hit and run attacks. Locally, another of their jobs was to recover aircrew who had been obliged to ditch their damaged aircraft in the North Sea and the Channel.

28,000 Pilll box fortifications were built to defend Britain in the case of invasion during WW2. They came in a variety of shapes, round, square, six or eight sided and between 15" and 3' 0" thick depending on their vulnerability. Many have been destroyed, the remainder left to remind us of those historic years when this country stood alone against Germany's second attempt to dominate Europe.

At the end of our road lived an elderly lady, Mrs Peynton, who had a two foot long preserved turtle hanging by a long cord against her stairwell wall. She assured me that when it heard the clock strike twelve the turtle climbed to the top of the cord but forgot to say that as well as being dead it also had defective hearing.

She also had a very much alive nephew, Colonel Menzies, who taught my brother cousin and myself to swim after the war was over. As a colonel of the newly formed Commandoes he had led raids on the French coast, to wipe out machine gun posts and other defences set up by the Germans on the cliff tops. This involved climbing the cliffs in the dark and then silently cutting the throats of the guards before causing as much mayhem and damage to the German defences as possible before retreating fast. He told me sadly that on every raid he had lost men, but luckily escaped death himself. Not for want of trying, when he stripped for swimming he bore the scars of many bullet wounds about his body. On one of these night raids he was dropped off close to the French coast at high speed in a rubber dinghy so that any enemy hearing the sound of the MGB would not suspect an attack due because of a changed note in the engine noise. Experiencing trouble during the attack he and what was left of his team failed to rendezvous in time for their pickup and spent the next few days adrift in the North Sea. They were finally rescued by luck by an MGB searching for a crashed aircrew.

30

Air raid tunnels

During 1939, anticipating the war, Ramsgate had been the first town in the country to dig deep air raid shelters. Two miles long, they were cut through the chalk between 18 and 22 metres below the surface and had 23 entrances so that nobody had to go more than a quarter of a mile to get to one. Our entrance was just inside Ellington Park, about 100 metres from our house. When enemy planes were sighted or heard, the Air Raid Wardens would telephone those towns expected to lie in the path of the planes and the siren was sounded. It was switched on and off repeatedly to make a wailing sound. To this day, if I hear that sound on films, it sends shivers down my spine and the hairs on the back of my neck rise. I have spoken to other people of my age and they all say they get the same feeling. Evidently the idea of being killed is quite unappealling even for a three year old child.

Being on the coast Ramsgate lacked the early warning that towns further inland enjoyed. Aircraft spotters needed several bearings to plot the probable course of enemy planes and their likely targets and allow time for air raid sirens to warn them. We had more rush. Folk did not worry about what to wear down an air raid tunnel, people arrived in a hurry in whatever they happened to have on, or sometimes in the middle of the night, what they were not wearing, a coat slipped on over a nightdress or pyjamas. I was just able to dress myself. If the siren sounded at night I had to put on a pullover and my shorts and pull on my Welling-ton boots while my mother wrapped up my baby brother and dressed herself. My father was absent as he was on fire duty. We then ran to the end of the road in company with our neighbours and down the steps into the damp smelling, chalk tunnel carrying our little folding chairs, X framed things with canvas seats, and a torch, *(see icon)* remember there was no street lighting. The tunnel widened out in places so that there was space to unfold the seats where we could and sit and wait until the "all clear" siren sounded its long steady howl, then we all climbed the stairs and went hurrying home again hoping that the house would still be there.

On the other side of the park, below the cellar of my Grandpa Drake's large Queen Anne house, was a tunnel which he had had dug through the chalk during WWl following a bombing raid by a German Zeppelin airship. It had a widened area where we could sit during a raid and another exit in the back garden lawn in case the house was hit, blocking the cellar exit. It smelled a bit musty but we could take a cushion or pillow to make things more comfortable. The shelter was frequently shared by Forces personnel who had taken advantage of the games room and facilities my grandfather had set aside at one end of the house for those stationed locally who attended the Methodist Church of which he was a very active member. We had electric light down there but for emergency there were also torches and a paraffin storm lantern. There are a number of houses in and around the town with tunnels below them, probably old smugglers tunnels, but I don't know of any other house with one specifically for air raids. In general, unlike London and the major ports and industrial centres, our raids were mostly, but not always, short affairs. Hit and run or a bomber turned back for some reason, perhaps damaged by gunfire, before dropping its load.

Waiting for the "All clear" siren in my grandfather's air raid cellar.

Callup and Restricted occupations

Most men between eighteen and forty-five were obliged to join the Forces, however some were refused because of course many jobs required skilled engineers, specialist knowledge, or provided necessary services. My father was one such, in what was called a Restricted Occupation. Our family business supplied bakers throughout Kent with everything except flour which came direct from the millers. Deliveries up to that point had been partly by motor vans and locally by horse drawn van. All the able bodied men were called up leaving my father to manage the yard and deliveries as best he could with one handicapped man, and others too old for military service plus my grandfather who was by then in his seventies. Restricted Tradesmen had to serve in other ways. My father being a reserve fireman before the actual outbreak of war was often on duty when he was not working as were Bill Matthews, our coalman and a friend, Mr Darby, the local pork butcher.

I have often wondered whether those men suffered any stigma because they were not in uniform most of the time. It was often the case that men not in the armed forces because of their beliefs, religious objectors, or handicapped in some way were subjected to taunts and bitter remarks from women whose husbands were serving overseas, or had been killed, or wounded, not understanding that men in Restricted Trades had no choice in the matter and were vital to the running of the nation. My father never spoke of it and I never thought to ask him. It may be he never had the problem as he had been born in the town and was very well known both as a sportsman, employer and churchman.

England needed aluminiun for the construction of more aircraft like this 1940 Spitfire which, with the Hurricane, was responsible for British success in the Battle of Britain.

Scrap metal for tanks and aircraft

Because of the shortage of materials necessary for the defence of the country all non essential garden and park railings were cut off and carted away to be melted down and re-used in the manufacture of armaments. Ramsgate trams had become redundant with the introduction of motor buses, and it may be that the need of steel for armaments induced the council to take up the old tramlines around the town at that time. I do know I was a bit frightened by the noise of the compressed air jackhammers used to break them out of the road. Women were asked to donate any old aluminiun saucepans so that the metal could be used for making aircraft. Both reduced the danger to the shipping otherwise needed to tranport ore from abroad.

Hairy Aunts and other titles

As a child I had several great uncles and a plethora of great aunts. It was difficult to distinguish between the aunts as, although individually related to one, or other, of my grandparents, they had in common a standard dress sense. Navy blue dresses with white polka dots, admittedly some had larger dots than others. All wore hats held on securely with long steel hat pins rammed through their hat and hair which was usually worn in a bun. Their physique varied from tall and thin to short and very comfortable, some were a trifle whiskery and I suspect shaved to overcome the problem making their fond kisses a bit bristly and unwelcome. As children we remembered them best for the size of the coins they gave us when they left. It was the custom of those times to give a present to children seen rarely; a little addition to our meagre money boxes. Sixpence or a shilling (twelve pence). To put that into perspective tu'pence (just under 1p in our present money) would buy a Mars bar. A field worker picking potatoes would earn ten shillings a day, just 50p.

One aunt who was not really an aunt at all, just a particular friend of my mother's family, broke all bounds and gave us half a crown, two shilling and six pence (twelve and a half new pence). We never forgot Auntie Nancy. It was common practice to call close friends of ones parents uncle or auntie, never ever just by their Christian name.

The whole business of names has undergone an enormous change during my lifetime. At school, at least in boys' schools, we were called by our surname and called most of our contemporaries by their surname, or a nickname. Drake became Drakey, Smith became Smithy, although one unfortunate boy in my class was cruelly, though with great justification, called Smelly. White became Chalky, Miller changed to Dusty. This habit followed through to adult life where business-men who had formerly been at school together continued to address one another in like fashion even in correspondence. I went through my schooling without ever knowing the first name of many others in my class. Men and women otherwise addressed each other formally as Mr or Mrs whatever their name happened to be. Familiarity was not encouraged and the formality could normally only be broken by the older person telling the younger their Christian name and that they could in future use it.

Shop assistants in the past would address their customers as Sir, Madam or Miss. Now pimply sixteen year olds freely call me Mate. I am not at all sure I wish to be mates with them, nor that they really wish to be one of mine, but to be sure I realise this is a management deficiency, not the fault of the uneducated young person.

There is an interesting comment by John Stewart Collis in his book "Down to Earth" published in 1947 which gives some insight to attitudes of the period. *"I call a gentleman, after knowing him a bit, simply 'Jones'; I call a lower-middle-class person 'Mr Jones', otherwise he is indignant, for he regards the Mr as his only title to fame; and with the working man I take a flying leap as soon as possible to the Christian name."*

Life with my grandparents

As a German invasion seemed probable, Ramsgate, being a port in sight of the French coast, was likely to become a prime target for attack. We moved to Sandwich, a largely Tudor town of no particular strategic importance, to live with my Cain grandparents. My father came over as often as his work, or fire station duties allowed. He had a heavy old iron bicycle with no gears and the journey of about seven miles must have been pretty miserable during the winter months. He had the use of his father's car, but petrol rationing had been introduced limiting driving to about 200 miles per month. By the following summer there was no petrol for private motorists, most were laid up until the end of the war. The time spent with my grandparents is a treasured memory.

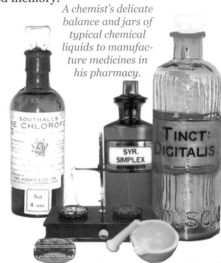

A chemist's delicate balance and jars of typical chemical liquids to manufacture medicines in his pharmacy.

This grandfather was a native of the Isle of Man. A quiet, serious and deeply religious man, some six feet tall and solidly built. He was the town's chemist with his tiny Tudor pharmacy at 24a King Street sharing street frontage with Mr Benstead's news agency, but full width at the rear with the dispensary, kitchen and scullery. On the upper floors were the livingroom, bedrooms and attic. On the other side an elderly lady ran a sweet shop which also sold icecream. Mr Benstead also had a stall at the station where Mother took me each week to buy a comic called Chicks Own.

Allenbury's throat lozenges and a pestle and mortar in which to grind ingredients for pills.

After my mother's marriage in 1934, her father had bought a new three bedroom house with a good size garden for about £800. It was just below the Mill Wall on the outside of the now dry moat which had in earlier times protected the town. His garden contained fruit trees and the brick lodge behind the house had the most delightful smell of stored apples and pears laid out on wooden racks, fruit that, together with blackberries and rhubarb, was bottled by my grandmother for use in pies during the winter.

They had bought one of the Government's Anderson bomb shelters for £7 (issued free to people earning less than £250 p.a.) and interred it in the slope down to the moat then covered it with earth in which he planted cabbages. When I asked him why he was planting them he said it was so the Germans would not discover where we were hiding. The real reason was a new law requiring anyone owning one to have it built, dug in and covered by the 11th June 1939 so that should a bomb land nearby, the blast would pass over it. After the war many people dug them out and used them as garden sheds on their allotments. You may still find them: practical, but not a thing of beauty.

THE ANDERSON SHELTER

An Anderson shelter could protect six people. 6'6" long x 4'6" wide x 6'0" high (2m x 1.35m x 1.8m), they were formed from several sheets of specially fabricated corrugated iron bent in the shape of the letter "J". Turned upside down the curved sections were bolted together to form an inverted "U". Flat sheets of the same material being used for the two ends, one of which had a door opening. The one illustrated has yet to have its door attached.

I suppose that my grandparents had intended to retire at this point, Grandpa was after all 74 years of age the year war broke out. He would probably have retired much earlier had he not lost a very considerable amount of money invested in chemical companies in Russia. These had been grabbed by the Communist state following the Russian revolution in 1919 and he had suffered a nervous breakdown as a result of all the worry associated with it.

The Blackout

Born in 1865 he was already too old to join the army for the First World War. Instead he had served in the Home Guard, later immortalised after WW2 by the TV series "Dad's Army" which, in both wars, was formed to help defend the country in the event of invasion. The start of another war that called up all the younger men for military service would have left the town without a pharmacy. He clearly felt it was his duty to continue and added to that also became an Air Raid Precautions Warden. Known as ARP wardens, these 1.4 million part time, unpaid men patrolled the completely unlit streets at night to warn anybody showing any light from their windows to "Put out that light". They were responsible for the distribution of Anderson and later Morrison shelters, the upkeep of public shelters, also with issuing gas masks that, like the new identity cards, folk were supposed to carry at all times. They were trained to take control until the fire brigade and other services arrived following an air raid. Their other duty was to assist the victims of an attack and render first aid. To assist them in all this they had only a steel helmet with ARP in white on the front of it, a pair of overalls with an armlet and a handbell with which to summon attention.

Each household throughout the country was obliged to fit lightproof shutters or blackout curtains to windows every evening so that the town would not be easily found by enemy bombers. Car and bicycle lights had shades fitted to deflect their beams down onto the road to minimise their presence. There was no street lighting, on moonless nights town and country were pitch black as the population groped about with only the aid of a torch when absolutely necessary and batteries did not last long. Indeed, it was the blackout that finally terminated Grandpa's career. On his way home after a night on duty and nearing eighty, he missed his footing on the steps up to the Mill Wall which runs above the moat ditch, fell and broke his leg so badly his foot was back to front.

He was a very educated man, the youngest son of a wealthy Manx architect and builder and unlike me, won many prizes of books at school; I still have some of them. He could read and understand French, German, Latin and Greek, was very interested in astronomy and art. He was the only man I've met who had ploughed his way through the whole of Edward Gibbon's "The Decline and Fall of the Roman Empire". (Written with all the dash and excitement of a serious Cromwellian scholar of the 1600s.) His great-grandfather had been an early member of the Methodist Church in the Isle of Man and had entertained John Wesley, its founder, in his home both in 1777 and again in 1780. The family remained staunch Methodists until my disaffection broke the tradition.

It was my grandparents' habit to rise at 6.30am and breakfast early to allow time for a Bible reading, plus extensive prayers for all and sundry before the day got under way. One hell of a drag for a four year old! A similar though not quite so lengthy programme was enacted at my other grandparents although at home my father modified things further to just a short Bible reading at breakfast and saying Grace at the start of all meals. The working day started at 8am for almost everybody and finished for most at 12 noon on Saturday. A standard 48 hour working week.

Sunday School

In those days far more people attended a church. Even if they did not, they frequently sent their children to Sunday School, either to better them, or to get them out of the way for a bit of peace and quiet on a Sunday afternoon. There was not a lot of either at the time, what with the war and the much longer working week. My first experience of Sunday School was during the Sandwich interlude. One Saturday the church had a fete at which there was a bran tub. A sort of lucky dip where the prizes were hidden in sawdust or bran (the flaky outer part of the wheat usually fed to horses). There was also a tub in which apples floated, the challenge was to get the apple in your mouth without using your hands; all frightfully jolly stuff for a Saturday afternoon. On Sunday I suppose my parents thought I was old enough to join in the service though not to stay for the sermon. At that point all the children went to an adjoining room for Sunday School where we had a story which I completely misunderstood, probably wasn't listening, but it involved a tub and apple. At that point I perked up and at lunch told my parents the subject of the lesson. Years later I realised that in fact the lesson had been about the tabernacle in which Moses was to guard God's laws.

INDIAN
LINIMENT

C. & D. Diary,   1917.

INVALUABLE FOR
Rheumatism, Neuralgia,
Sciatica, Sprains,
Lumbago, Cramp, Stiff Joints,
&c., &c.

DIRECTIONS.

Gently rub the affected part with the
liniment until it penetrates, relieving
all pain and giving a feeling of warmth
and comfort.

J. H. CAIN M.P.S Chemist
24a, King Street
SANDWICH,

The Pharmacy

Behind the pharmacy the building was divided into two rooms, a kitchen and Grandpa's dispensary. Both the dispensary and the shop were lined with wooden drawers with Latin names on each and shelves with large flasks of coloured liquids. Few medicines came pre-packed although I recall Cow & Gate baby food and supplies of Allenbury's cod liver oil and malt with which we were dosed each day after breakfast. Many years later this was still available. I bought some for my first child and took a spoon-full, remembering how I used to like it. Cod liver oil is definitely an acquired taste and somewhere over the intervening years I had well and truly lost it.

There were also cough pastilles in green tins that I recall because my father used the old tins to store nails and screws, indeed I still have one somewhere in my workshop. Pills and medicines were mostly made up by the chemist; the ingredients carefully measured out on a delicate brass balance, hand ground using a pestle and mortar then poured into bottles or pressed into moulds to make pills. The photo above was taken in my grandfather's previous shop in Hove that, like Brighton, enjoyed the patronage of the aristocracy, who often enjoyed visiting the seaside to take the fresh sea airs for health reasons. Unfortunately this class of gentry, while believing they should have a first rate service, did not always believe in parting with their cash in a hurry, sometimes waiting a year or more, or until they needed a fresh supply before paying for the last lot. Indeed, some never came back adding to his already serious financial problems. As a result of these troubles he had moved to the quiet of Sandwich for a less exotic life.

Shopping

Another memory of this period is shopping with Grandma. Supermarkets were still many years away. We would go to Mr Rose's grocery store and order what was required. Mr Rose and his assistants stood behind the long mahogany counter which separated the customers from the goods. *(See icon)* Choice was simple, much less choice than today. Basics like tea, coffee, butter, margarine, lard, sugar, two, or three, different cheeses, Jacobs cream crackers and various sweet biscuits, jams and tinned meat, fish, fruit, Kellogs cornflakes and Scott's

A trades bike. Often loaded so heavily that it was difficult to get off without it tipping up before the front legs could be lowered. I speak from my own experience.

porridge oats. (Porridge was Grandpa's chosen daily starter, sprinkled with salt instead of sugar). Bacon was cut on the spot by a hand wound red and chrome machine, the action of which fascinated me. Absolutely nothing in pre-wrapped plastic packets.

Very few people had cars and clearly could not carry all this home with them. It would be delivered later by an errand boy on a heavy trades bike that had a large pannier over the front wheel. The same applied at the butcher. One ordered the meat, which would be delivered later with a small, slightly bloody bill detailing the weight and price pinned to it by a short, sword shaped wire. This would be paid at the next visit. I don't think my mother ever carried meat home, except during our

stay in Lamberhurst, where we were too far out of the village for it to be delivered. It may also be that there was nobody to ride the bike anyway, or the joint so small it could easily be carried in her shopping basket. It is interesting to note that a few of the great super-market groups and large stores are now offering home delivery services again. That may be the way of the future, as traffic congestion rises it may be preferable to have a few delivery vehicles rather than streets solid with private cars.

Automatic door closers now replace the older shop door system. This sort of change does not get recorded in history books. In this picture you will see that the point of the metal bracket on top of the door supports one end of the weighted cord and also hits the bell as the door is opened warning the shopkeeper of a customer's arrival when busy doing housework in the back room.

Our first Air Raid

The first air raid on Sandwich happened while we were staying there. We heard a great explosion and a lot of gunfire. A bit later, walking with my grand-mother to the town, we passed St Clement's Church where two excited soldiers, who had an anti-aircraft gun mounted on top of its tower, shouted down to us that a bomb had narrowly missed the Barbican Toll bridge and landed on the opposite side of the river towards Ramsgate. The depression it made in the soft mud of the river bank was later infilled with concrete and turned into a slipway for small boats so proved quite useful.

Living day to day

For me the war fell into the background for a time, the only difference was that we were in Sandwich and my father was missing for a lot of the time. My grandmother helped to keep me entertained and it was in her home that I spent my only white Christmas. The message is "Don't waste your money at the bookmakers betting on a white Christmas." The odds for me have been 78-1 against, however I did enjoy it. My grandmother had been brought up in a small village where her grandfather had been a farmer. She liked baking and fresh food. Indeed at the time people in general had no choice in the matter, there was no frozen food in the home so they ate whatever was in season or stored from the garden.

My only white Christmas

Take-aways and packaged food did not exist except for tinned or dried food, like Heinz soups or cornflakes. Icecream had been available in the shop to be eaten before it melted but not for home storage. Grandpa grew a lot of his vegetables and fruit. I accompanied my grandmother into the field between her home and Sir Roger Manwood's School to collect mushrooms and learn the difference between them and toadstools. Mr Hooker, a professional gardener, lived next door and gave her his surplus produce.

Saturday mornings had an unvaried routine both at home and at my grandmother's. It was baking day and it was my great pleasure to assist. My major contribution being licking the jam spoon and making sure the newly baked tarts tasted correct. Every week it was the same, a large fruit or rhubarb pie, several trays of raspberry jam tarts and best of all a pastry man cut out with a metal mould. I could then decorate him with currants for his eyes, nose, mouth and buttons. If any pastry was left it made a jam turnover. Pastry at that time was made with butter or margarine and lard. This was then stored in the larder, a cool, well ventilated cupboard below the stairs on the north side of the house. It always had a mouth watering raspberry smell. I cannot remember anyone having a domestic refrigerator before the war. The pastry's fat content would horrify a modern dietician and my cardiologist, but those were the materials available though it was doubtlessly modified as the rationing system took hold. Except for the war years my grandmother managed to eat it all her life but not to excess and survived to one hundred and three. Well into her teens before the invention of the motor car, she lived to see the first man land on the moon, live, on television.

On the next page there is another photo of me with my next birthday present. A bus conductor's outfit which brought to mind the equipment used by conductors of that epoch. He sold the tickets. Double decker buses had no door at the back, just an open platform so people could get on and off freely. One paid the conductor who, as the bus moved off, would call out a warning to those customers still standing, then ring the bell to tell the driver to go. So it went like this, "Hold very tight please" Ding ding. The driver only drove so the bus stopped for less time. He sat isolated in his cab on all buses.

The conductor collected the fare during the journey so stoppages were short. He had a leather pouch for money, a clip board of various priced tickets and like me, a machine that punched a hole in them so they could not be used again. Buying train tickets was also a quick affair, For instance one might say "Single to Chatham please." The booking office clerk would take a ticket from the Chatham column of his ticket rack and flip it through the little arched window of his office in return for payment. About twenty seconds per customer. Now we wait in long queues while the man at his computer asks where you wish to go, pause while he feeds this into his machine. "Which day", another pause, "1st or 2nd class", "reservation or not," " facing forwards or backwards...." It goes on and on and all the waiting queue fidget and tut and look at their watches and count again the number of people in front of them.

Laundry

A copper was the washing machine of the epoch. It was a brick built fireplace in the corner of the scullery with a large copper bowl above, about 60cm diameter, in a bricked surround up to its rim. A coal fire was lit below and the whole would become very hot, the brickwork acting as insulation to retain the heat. Monday was washing day throughout Britain. Not necessarily the only wash day but the main one with last week's dirty clothes and the bed linen. Babies nappies were all of towelling and were washed daily. Drip-dry and non-iron materials had yet to be invented. Wool, linen and cotton ruled. Boiled in the copper, passed through the mangle to get out as much water as possible, rinsed and mangled twice or more then hung out to dry on Monday, in fine weather on the line and in wet on a clothes horse in front of the fire or hoisted up on a rack to the kitchen or living room ceiling. *(See illustration on p108)* Drying and ironing occupied Tuesday and Wednesday.

Because of the time and expense of using hot water, rinsing was done using cold water with a sugar lump size of blue dye shaken in a sort of closed tea strainer. Used in moderation this helped to emphasise the whiteness of white washing. Summer and winter this was performed under her roofed, open sided shed behind the scullery and the building's only toilet. Outside toilets were common as many people thought it unhygienic to have one inside. Laundry was hard work in summer and freezing cold in winter. Women's fingers became sore, cracked and bled from chilblains caused by the cold water. Her ironing

For those who could afford it laundry baskets were collected each week when the previous week's wash was returned and paid for to the van driver from their local steam laundry.

was still done with what were called flat irons. Shaped more or less like those used today, they were heated on top of the kitchen range and used in rotation. When the heat was used up they went back on the range again. My mother, com

paratively newly married, had an electric iron. Rain on Mondays and Tuesdays was a real pain what with being unable to get close to the fire and the plop, plop, plop of water dripping into strategically positioned bowls and the risk of a smack in the face from wet pullovers and knickers hanging from a ceiling frame. When dried outside in the fresh air clothes always smelt nicer.

A copper and its equipment. So called because the bowl set into the brick surround was made of copper.

The well to do and single men had their washing collected each week by commercial laundries. It would be returned the following week in exchange for the next lot. Others used them in dire necessity, but most women did their own until the 1960s. By then the war had changed life, many women had become accustomed to a degree of financial independence.

Another factor was that life had become more sophisticated. There was comparatively full employment. New aids to a fuller life were appearing in the shops. Television had burst onto the scene, greatly boosted by the desire to watch the young Queen Elizabeth's coronation in 1953, its influence driving the public's aspirations.

The first laundry improvement I recall was a Flatly Drier, a worktop high, white metal box with a lid but no bottom. The washing was hung over wooden slats just below the lid and was dried by a heating element at the bottom. In 1959 my brother and I bought one for our parents to mark their Silver Wedding anniversary. About this time John Bloom bought the Rolls Razor Company and used it to start direct selling of twin tub washing machines. The Government had recently relaxed regulations to allow hire purchase. This, added to a price well below his competitors, gave Bloom a ready market for a few years. The company went bust in 1964. At the time I was running a direct selling sales team and attended the creditors meeting to contact the sales force who were owed commission by Rolls hoping to recruit them for my force. Bloom had weekly told them that they were the cream of the country's direct salesmen and its highest earners. Curiously they believed him.

At the point my story started there were plenty of newer, lighter, rubber roller mangles on the market. This enormous beast had worn wooden rollers but, like so many things, was a leftover from the Victorian age and built to last, as was my grandmother who owned it.

43

Looking at their individual commission slips it was clear they lived largely on their belief in the words of John Bloom. Fifteen joined me, but a couple of months later only two were still in my force. Although John Bloom's organisation collapsed it had done British women an enormous favour forcing down the price of white goods to affordable levels.

I digress...back to my grandmother.

This is not exactly the same as my grandmother's range. Here you see the water is heated in a cast iron container on top of the oven. Her cooker had it in place of one of the ovens. There were many designs available. At night the fire basket front could be covered to slow the burning and survive till morning.

The black, cast iron cooking range was in the kitchen. It stood in what had been the chimney in Tudor times. To one side there was the oven and on the other a hot water tank with a brass tap while the centre section was the coke, or coal fired, stove with hot plates over it where the pots were cooked. The fire basket was comparatively small but with the mass of cast iron round it to distribute the heat it made a very efficient cooker, water and room heater all in one.

The big London stores like Gamages and the Army and Navy Store still had a considerable selection of ranges in their catalogues throughout the 30's. I was very interested to see it because we had a gas cooker at home as did my grandmother in her new house. Upstairs was larger than the ground floor with bedrooms, a dining room and sitting room which extended over Mr Benstead's shop and looked down on the street.

Having had two daughters, but no sons, my grandmother had no experience of bringing up small boys so she taught me what she had previously taught them. I therefore learnt to knit. I believe that to this day I could cast on stitches, knit plain and pearl and cast off. She showed me how to do embroidery, chain stitch, lazy daisy, and hemming, also how to darn a hole and stitch round a buttonhole. I knitted a cardigan for my teddy bear but when dressing him got a bit confused about which holes were for buttons, which for arms and which were just dropped stitches. However they say nothing one learns is wasted and certainly the stitching came in very useful many years later when repairing the sails of my boat and making shirts. In the 50's and 60's, being tall, I had considerable trouble finding long shirts, there then being no XL size, so I made them, otherwise I was obliged to resort to a size eighteen collar in which, being skinny, I looked ridiculous.

One of Grandma's acquaintances was a Mr Offen who had a drapery shop on the corner of the market square. I viewed a visit there with mixed feelings. Without exception he would pat me heavily on the head and say: "Your Grandma spoils you doesn't she". Every time, like a record. On the other hand I loved to watch the mechanical system attached to the shop ceiling by which each assistant was able to fire a small metal cup containing the bill and the customer's money along twin wires direct to the central cash desk. The cashier in her glass windowed cabin then unscrewed the cup from its carrier with a half twist, removed the contents, placed the receipted bill and any change in the cup, pulled a trigger and fired it back to the shop assistant. Very simple and efficient. Neither the customer, cashier or assistant had to move at all. Many larger drapery stores had this system.

Hospital

It was during our time in Sandwich that I had to have my tonsils removed. This was done at Deal hospital and another sixty-four years were to pass before I needed to make another hospital visit for myself. I remember very little of the event except having a mask placed over my face and being told count to ten and a few days later being taken to Jenner's toy shop, a few doors away from my grandfather's pharmacy, to choose a present for my heroism (or not making too much fuss) during the operation. I received a level crossing for my clockwork Hornby 'O' guage railway set. Hornby had introduced their 'OO' guage trains the previous year but of course I was too young for one. Production of "OO" gauge was then put on hold until the war was over and not restarted until 1948. The removal of tonsils and adenoids was then very common, but is much more rare nowadays due to the use of antibiotics.

Evacuation

The 28-30 May 1940 witnessed the Dunkirk evacuation. There had been an evacuation of Londoners when war first broke out, but as there had been no serious raids many had filtered back to their homes. This was different. The enemy were in sight from Dover and Ramsgate. With the rapid advance of the Germans and capitulation of the French, the British Expeditionary Force soldiers had to be rescued from France and were heroically aided by many boats, large and small, naval and private.

Two survivors of the dramatic rescue in Ramsgate Harbour, RNLI lifeboat William and Kate Johnston and MV Sundowner.

Ramsgate was one of the principle ports to which these men returned, exhausted from fighting for days and nights on end with almost no sleep. My father told me many were marching exhausted, their eyes shut, a lot wounded and in a very bad way. (I later worked with a limping man who had been wounded in the leg and was towed across the Channel in a lifebelt as there was no room in the boat.) It was expected the Germans would immediately follow them across the sea and the Ramsgate region would become a forward fighting area and extremely dangerous. Almost all the Ramsgate children were moved away by train wearing a large identification label dangling from their necks. Most went to Utoxeter in Staffordshire having said sad goodbyes to their parents, or frequently just their mothers as many men were already doing Military Service.

Children from Kent being evacuated, each with a label around his or her neck, a small suitcase and their gas mask in the small boxes. On arrival they were to be selected by their new carers, like sheep in a market, children of the same family often split up.

On 1 June 1940 we left Ramsgate forgetting my favourite toy, the fire red engine, in my toy cupboard.

Our destination was Lamberhurst, to live in a semi-detached cottage, 2 Wayside, in Furnace Lane, so called because it had formerly led to an iron works that made, among other things, the railings for St Paul's Cathedral. It was found for us by an aunt who ran a village grocery store on the Common. I found the move quite exciting, but it must have been an extremely worrying time for my parents when my father had to leave us two days later. He was returning to the danger zone and my parents had no idea what the future held for them. What if there was an invasion and the south of the country was quickly overrun by the enemy? How could they keep in touch in such an emergency as telephone and postal services would probably be damaged or destroyed?

We moved to the country where I saw a scarecrow and single decker buses for the first time. I drew this as a present to send my father.

Shelling

The Germans installed huge guns on the French coast capable of lobbing large shells across the Channel and doing vast damage to Dover and to a lesser extent to Ramsgate being at the limit of their range. I recall walking with my grandfather along Ramsgate's West Cliff, near the Paragon, to show me where a shell had just cleared the top of the cliff and damaged the basement of a house. A number had landed in the lower regions of the town. From the top of the cliff we could see the huge flash from the guns in France as they fired at poor old Dover. This must have been either during our stay in Sandwich, or a holiday after our evacuation to Lamberhurst.

Evacuation did not stop with people. Our family business had changed from horse drawn deliveries to motors, only retaining one animal, "Molly" for local calls. The shelling terrified the poor creature so she too was evacuated, to a farm near Cranbrook. By the time the war was over she was too old for work and ended her days there to the regret of my grandfather, a great horse lover, some of the older staff and myself.

Essential businesses were also put on standby to evacuate. The following pages are instructions from the government's Ministry of Food to my grandfather detailing the steps he was to take in the event of invasion.

Around 1936: "Molly" winning first place in a carnival for Best Trades Float. My grandfather in bowler hat and wearing a buttonhole. Note the vast proportion of people are wearing hats.

A secret Government Directive

MINISTRY OF FOOD
South Eastern Divisional Food Office,
Manor House, Bishop's Down, Tunbridge Wells, Kent.

SECRET

EVAC/WHOLE

June 15th, 1942.

Dear Sirs,

Compulsory Evacuation Scheme.

As the result of further information which we have received from the Head-quarters of the Ministry at Colwyn Bay, since the meetings at Canterbury and Brighton, and which is set forth below, I am writing this letter to make the position clear. You will observe that their families will not be allowed to accompany the staff to the alternative premises.

As you are probably aware, arrangements are being made for the compulsory evacuation of the inhabitants of certain coastal towns, of which yours is one, should invasion appear to be imminent.

If the evacuation should take place, only a nucleus of people will be left behind to carry on the Civil Defence, etc. Services and it will not be possible for you to continue your business in the town. It has accordingly been arranged with the Ministry of Home Security and the Regional Commissioner concerned that you shall be permitted to move to premises elsewhere whence you will be able to continue to serve your retail customers outside the town. It will be necessary for you to remove your stocks to the alternative premises within a week of notice being given and also to take with you your transport and such of your staff as you consider to be necessary to enable you to give adequate service from your new address.

You will, in due course, receive a notice from the Chief Constable under Defence Regulation 16A, directing you to remove to the alternative premises upon receipt of instructions from the Police and to move your transport and such of your stocks as may be designated by the Food Executive Officer or his agent.

It will be necessary to serve a similar notice on each member of your staff whom you decide should accompany you instead of being evacuated with the main body of townsfolk. Will you please furnish me as soon as possible with a list of names and addresses of each member of the staff whom you decide should accompany you and the address of the alternative premises. As far as possible female employees should be allowed to go with the main body of evacuees. The family of any member of the staff chosen to accompany you will be evacuated with the main body unless they have previously moved out of the town of their own accord. If you have already furnished the required informa-tion, I shall treat it as an answer to this letter unless I hear from you to the contrary.

-1-

You should note that if you are required under Defence Regulation 16A to remove your stocks the Government can accept no liability for any expenses you may incur. If, however, for reasons beyond your control it is not possible for you to move the stocks you should inform the Food Executive Officer who, if he decides that it is impossible for you to comply with the Order, will give you a notice in writing to that effect and at his discretion will requisition the stocks and arrange for them to be moved. If the stocks are requisitioned compensation will be payable under the provision of the Compensation (Defence) Act.

Emergency petrol coupons will be given to you to enable you to move your transport and stocks.

Yours faithfully,

M. C. R. Lidal.

Deputy Divisional Food Officer.

To Wholesalers in Evacuation Towns.

Baldwin Hughes & Drake Ltd

This document is interesting for a number of reasons apart from its message:

It shows that the Government was still expecting an invasion almost three years after the outbreak of war.

It illustrates how sudden necessary changes in a war can completely disrupt the lives of the population who will then be treated like sheep. All decisions taken without any reference to their personal wishes.

It is printed on poor grade paper, almost without margins to make maximum use of the material which was in very short supply. I recall that the stalks of stinging nettles were added to the mix in papermaking to supplement the normal range which had included wood chip from Scandinavia. This was no longer available and any wood in Britain was needed for aircraft, boats, furniture and building repairs.

Even the heading of the paper is typewritten because speed of communication did not allow time for new departments to wait for the production of printed matter.

It is also evidence of the quality of typewriters of the period, some letters being damaged (Note the capital A for instance). Also the pressure exerted by the typist varies. Very different from the later golfball electric machines of the early 60s or present day computer output. All printing was letterpress, not today's offset litho.

Form W.H.C.3.   Licence No......1456.............

MINISTRY OF FOOD.

LICENCE.

To.......BALDWIN,...HUGHES...&...DRAKE...LTD.,..........................

...........BRADSTONE...STORES,...BRADSTONE...AVENUE,...................

...........FOLKESTONE,...KENT..

DEFENCE REGULATIONS 1939, AS AMENDED.
THE FOOD (RESTRICTION ON DEALINGS) ORDER, 1941.

    1. Pursuant to Article 2 of the above mentioned Order you are hereby authorised as from the date hereof, and until further notice to sell otherwise than by retail the specified food(s) mentioned in the Schedule to this Licence.

    2. This Licence may be revoked at any time and is not transferable.

(Sgd.)......*John Crah*......

For and on behalf of the Minister.

Dated   20th day of   OCTOBER   , 194 1.

THE SCHEDULE.

CANNED FRUIT.	FROZEN EGGS.
CANNED VEGETABLES.	JAM.
COFFEE ESSENCE(INCLUDING COFFEE	MARMALADE.
AND CHICORY ESSENCE).	MILK POWDER.
CORNFLOUR, BLANCMANGE POWDER	RICE.
AND CUSTARD POWDER.	SUGAR.
DRIED FRUITS.	SYRUP AND TREACLE.
EGG PRODUCTS.	

SO5290 M190/6048 8/41 20m C&R 703

Food Control

Strict controls were introduced to ensure the fair distribution of food. Only existing businesses qualified for a ration and these were given an area of responsibility which did not involve excessive fuel usage. The above licence was for the supply of bakery materials from our Folkestone depot and listed the rationed goods which we were permitted to handle. Coupons issued to the baker had to be submitted to his supplier without which he could not obtain further supplies of that product. For some reason butter was left off this licence but added on a separate licence a month later.

Egg products covered egg in various forms. Fresh eggs were in very short supply but supplemented by egg, which was frozen, flaked or dried also jerk which was simply broken, or cracked eggs emptied into a 7lb jar, sold only to trade customers. *(See icon)* Later, as shortages got more acute, bakers used egg colouring in buns and cakes. These contained no egg at all and came in two colours, a rather luminous pink and an unreal yellow both of which disguised the flour's greyness, but added nothing to the dry, almost flavourless cake except a cheerful colour.

50

MINISTRY OF FOOD.

Tel: 2740.
Central Public Library,
Grace Hill,
Folkestone.

20th November, 1940.

VERY IMPORTANT:

Dear Sir or Madam,

CIRCULAR NO. 33.

Will you please note that in the event of your stock or business premises being damaged as a result of enemy action, you should immediately notify me at this Office of the fact.

Yours faithfully,

Harold G. Wheeler

FOOD EXECUTIVE OFFICER.

HGW/PH

To All Retailers.

You will notice from the above that this branch of the Ministry of Food had taken over at least part of the Public Library as its offices and again there had been no time to arrange printing of notepaper.

War allows Government to take over, move and redistribute the use of any buildings, materials or people as it sees best in the national interest no matter how inconvenient for the individuals concerned.

Form W.H.C.3.
Licence No. BC/SE/2953.

MINISTRY OF FOOD.

LICENCE.

To Baldwin Hughes & Drake Ltd.

Bradstone Avenue,

Folkestone, Kent.

DEFENCE REGULATIONS 1939, AS AMENDED.
THE FOOD (RESTRICTION ON DEALINGS) ORDER, 1941.

1. Pursuant to Article 2 of the above mentioned Order you are hereby authorised as from the date hereof, and until further notice to sell otherwise than by retail the specified food(s) mentioned in the Schedule to this Licence.

2. This Licence may be revoked at any time and is not transferable.

(Sgd.) H. E. Davis

For and on behalf of the Minister.

Dated 19th day of November, 1941.

THE SCHEDULE.

National Butter.

51

First projects

Memories are very selective; one of mine is of sitting in the garden rockery of our new home in inland Lamberhurst, in the sunshine. Like many people I remember the sun shining most of my childhood, not the pouring rain, nor the sore backs of my bare legs where my wellington boots rubbed them raw. Coming from the seaside, I set about bashing pieces of the local sandstone together to produce sand to make sandcastles. I probably made several ounces before losing interest. I have always associated this memory with the sound of bees and RAF aircraft, both buzzing above me. I was also concerned for our safety following the air raid on Sandwich, so set about digging a tunnel down which I planned to save the family. Work proceeded to a depth of considerable inches before this project was also abandoned. The plastics industry was in its infancy and as drinking straws were just that, corn stalks, as we commonly call the stalks of wheat. Nothing to do with sweetcorn. With the outbreak of war, factories had much more important things to do than making drinking straws. By pushing my way through the hedge I remedied the shortfall with pair of scissors after harvesting finished by collecting as many unbroken stalks as possible and cutting them to length.

After harvest, fields were open to gleaners, an ancient right for anyone who had the time, patience or need to walk the fields and collect the remnants of the crop at no cost. Probably a spin-off caused by the romantic story of Ruth in the Bible. In the case of wartime cornfields people gathered seed heads and straw to care for feeding chicken and rabbits. Both were considered luxury items on anyones' dinner table.

New Neighbours

Mr and Mrs Chandler had moved in next door shortly after we settled there. I was fascinated by Mrs Chandler's appearance as the poor woman suffered from a considerably enlarged thyroid, a problem which made me think of a turkey. My first contact with her was when she lent over the fence and scolded me for bullying my younger brother by taking something away from him. Not withstanding this poor start we became good friends and maintained contact until the end of her life. Her elderly husband took a job as gardener to an admiral who had a substantial house set back from the Common. He used to cut the lawn with a scythe as neat as you could wish. I have seen many people using this tool and have done so myself on long grass or hay which both offer a bit of resistance, but cutting short grass with one presents a real challenge.

A right-handed scythe, normally about 5' 6" long. For left-handed people the handles can usually be reversed but they need a different blade. Requiring constant sharpening for razor clean cutting, the stone for this was usually carried on the user's belt. To get the best edge the stone had to be drawn away from the blades top side.

Corn harvesting

Behind our new home was a cornfield separated from the garden by a hedge with gaps large enough to admit small children. This was before the introduction during the 1950s, of combined harvesters, which break the straw during the threshing process. The reaping machines of the period were pulled by horse or tractor. They had a series of revolving arms which pulled the growing wheat towards them as it was cut off near the ground, feeding the parallel stalks onto a conveyor belt that whisked them towards the binding mechanism and tied them into fat, round sheaves. These the field workers stood in groups of five or six to await collection after they had finished drying. This could be after a few days, or a matter of some weeks, depending on the weather. These groups were called stooks. The cutting arm of the binder was mounted on one side of the machine so it had to start at the side of the field and keep going, in the same direction, spiral-ling slowly in towards the shrinking centre. Any animals hidden in the field would therefore keep moving into the remaining shelter of the crop rather than make a break for it across the already mown field. Towards the end of the work the farmer and workers would be standing around the clump that remained with their terriers and shot guns in the hope of getting a rabbit or hare for dinner when any unfortunate creatures finally made their break from cover.

Perhaps I should mention that the stalks of wheat and barley were considerably longer in those days, which caused far more crops to be beaten over by wind and heavy rain. After the war, shorter strains were to be developed which overcame this problem. The crop was also harvested a couple of weeks earlier than became normal after the introduction of the combined harvester. This was because the drying process while in stooks left the straw stronger and more pliable and suitable for thatching than is the case where the plant dries out before harvesting. Except for thatchers, this is no longer an important factor.

Collected in due course on a horse or tractor drawn trailer, the sheaves were carted to the farmyard, where they were built into ricks sometimes round, some-times rectangular, about ten feet high then up to a central point and finished with a roof of thatch to await the threshing machine, which would remove the grain and leave the stalks for bedding or, rarely by then, for thatching roofs. The sheaves were laid on their side in a circle perhaps twelve feet in diameter with the seed heads towards the centre which was left open to give ventilation for any residual damp to escape. The modern combined harvester does all this in one go using only two men, one to drive the machine and the other on a tractor pulling a trailer alongside it to catch the grain. The straw is only good for feed or bedding, no longer of any use for thatching. Notice I said on the tractor, at the time of the picture it was on a tractor, there was no inside, no cab or anti-roll bar.

HARVEST:

The painting overleaf of a late 1940s farm illustrates the changing techniques used for harvest-ing wheat, which we habitually called corn. Sweet corn was not then a well known crop in Britain. The farmer has changed to a Ferguson tractor which could do much more than a horse, however the reaping machine which was formerly horse drawn needing only one man now needed two for this particular operation. The tractor driver could not operate the cutter blade height on the reaper from that position. About this time the combined harvester was just making its debut. Note also the height of the corn, present day crops are considerably shorter and less prone to damage by wind and rain.

Women's Land Army

In the first six months of the war more than thirty thousand agricultural workers joined the forces. Because of the desperate shortage of men left to manage work normally done by them, the Government re-formed the Women's Land Army which had been instituted during WW1. Their uniform was a pair of brown knee breeches, green pullover and long socks. They were either housed in a hostel and allocated to a farm as needed or actually lived at a farm. For their long hours they received about £1. 12p per week plus their keep. The Land Girl at Ridge Farm, the farm opposite us, was

'We could do with thousands more like you..'

JOIN THE

WOMEN'S LAND ARMY

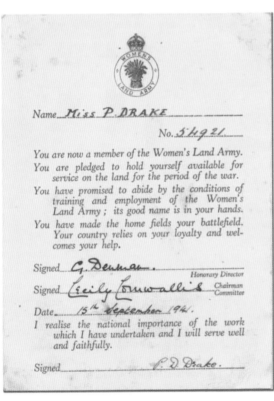

My cousin's Women's Land Army enrolment form

Name Miss P. DRAKE

No. 54921

You are now a member of the Women's Land Army.
You are pledged to hold yourself available for service on the land for the period of the war.
You have promised to abide by the conditions of training and employment of the Women's Land Army; its good name is in your hands.
You have made the home fields your battlefield. Your country relies on your loyalty and welcomes your help.

Signed _G. Denman._
                                        Honorary Director
Signed _Cecily Cornwallis_   Chairman
                                        'Committee
Date _15th September 1941._
I realise the national importance of the work which I have undertaken and I will serve well and faithfully.

Signed _P. D. Drake._

called Iris and I got to know her when I went to play with my school friend Basil. His father was the manager. Towards the end of the war Ralph Hazelden, the owner of Ridge Farm, returned having been released, or rescued from a German prisoner of war camp. He married my cousin whose parents had the grocery store on the opposite side of the Common. Many years later he retired and the farm became converted to a vineyard, one of the first in Britain. Another cousin, Pearl, also joined the Land Army and the photo on the next page shows her with others. A third, older cousin worked in a dairy. I was horrified as a small boy to hear that she had been injured when a cow suddenly swung its head round and put its horn through her cheek. Apparently this did not put her off milk as she later became a Milk Officer in Scotland. By 1944 there were 80,000 women working in agriculture.

On a cold winter morning these Land Girls have managed to get the tractor bogged down in a wet field. My cousin Pearl is the driver.

Italian Prisoners of War

The Land Army girls were not the only labour force available to farmers. With the defeat of the army of Italian dictator, Mussolini, there were many Italian prisoners of war held in camps around Britain, surrounded by barbed wire and guarded by the army. Many of the prisoners had been opposed to the war and hated their Fascist dictator. These men were released on a daily basis to various farms to assist if they were short handed. Quite a lot of them fell in love with English girls and when war finished returned to marry them and opened icecream parlours and restaurants adding the first taste of Mediterranean food to the staid English diet.

The execution of Mussolini was featured in all the newspapers, hanging by his feet with his wife. The first time I had seen a picture of a dead person, it had a gory fascination for me and is still available on the internet.

Village life

Wartime country life did not make daily chores any easier for my mother. Like our Ramsgate home this house had electricity but here there was no gas, or bathroom, and the toilet was attached to the back of the house, accessed from outside in common with millions of other homes.

Coal gas was produced in towns by a local gas works cooking coal in great ovens and pumping it at low pressure to the local popula-tion. Villages had to use another fuel. Bottled natural gas was a post-war innovation. Even in the late 80s while living in Woodchurch, near Ashford in Kent I was told: "Sorry Sir, I don't know the price of gas

This is the advertisement for our two ring paraffin cooker.

pipe per foot but you need six miles of it." In Lamberhurst we had a two ring paraffin cooker with an oven which took forever to get hot enough for baking. The paraffin was stored in a large glass container and fed to two wicks under the two rings.

There was no national standard power output between our many electricity generating companies. Radios need a precise standard output so were powered by accumulators, upright thick glass jars with a carrying handle. In it were metal plates and acid like a car battery. If one did not listen to the radio for too long, this battery would last a week. Every week therefore my mother had to cart a heavy accumulator and a paraffin can plus my two year old younger brother to the village where Mr Redman, the local garage owner, would refill the can and exchange the accumulator for a newly charged one.

Of course washing took a fair amount of her time. Baths were normally taken on Saturday evenings in a tin bath, in front of the fire in winter, and involved hours of heating water on the stove or in the wood fired copper.

An accumulator.

This model of a tin bath in use by a miner is actally made of coal by Collieryroad.com. There were several designs of galvanised iron baths. This one is typical, others were slight-ly longer, but perhaps used less as they needed more hot water.

Similar to that of my grandmother. All remnants of soap bars were carefully put into a wire framed contraption with a foot long, looped wire handle, like two large tea strainers face to face. This was shaken in the washing-up water as there was no other detergent.

Daffy

There was an old fellow we sometimes encountered on the Common looking after two harmless looking white goats he had staked out on it, exercising his Rights of Common. This was the ancient right of local people, the Commoners, to use certain land as grazing for a limited number of animals for a certain period of time. He introduced himself to my mother as Daffy Boreman. He was a real character "I'm stone deaf" he used to shout each time he met us, just in case we had forgotten. Then in case our memories were failing "I'm over ninety years old." That may well account for his disappearance not long after. They say "Pride comes before a fall", however not before one of his goats had butted my brother to the floor seconds after this picture was taken. He was offering the ungrateful beast a handful of bread.

Compulsory requisitions of property

With the vast expansion of the Forces and their urgent need for accommodation and office premises many houses were requisitioned by them. Others were taken for hospitals and maternity homes. There was no time to argue. The bombing resulted in many people becoming homeless. Wives in that situation and whose husbands were in the Forces had to reorganise their lives and those of their children, frequently without even being able to contact him. Phones were not mobile. Most people had no phone. Ringing someone overseas took a lot of arranging even in peacetime and anyway the Forces were not allowed to say where they were as the information might be valuable to the enemy. Returning Forces personnel could come home on leave and find a pile of bricks where their home formerly stood and then try to trace their family's new address.

To facilitate re-housing bombed out families the government took powers to lodge them with anyone who had been luckier and had a spare room or rooms. We had three bedrooms, but were using two so had a Mrs Hunt and her son Michael compusorily boarded on us for a period.

I believe her husband was a pilot. The arrangement was an uncomfortable one for all concerned. They did not have much in common with us and with such a lack of cooking facilities in the kitchen it must have been very trying for both women. My brother and I played together and I suspect, left the newcomer out of our games. His father got leave for Easter and brought his son an Easter egg and marzipan chicks, unavailable locally. We had ordinary eggs which we boiled in a pan with wood sorrel, onion and grasses to colour the shells. I must have been very jealous to remember such a trifling detail.

Tinkers and Gipsies

Periodically travelling people would call. Tinkers asking if one had knives or garden shears needing sharpening or saucepans requiring repair. They would park their specially adapted trades bike with its pedal driven grindstone in the lane and set to work. Many people still had kettles and pans made of iron which eventually broke or rusted through. They riveted handles back on or patched a hole. Gipsies would appear in the spring. They camped in a disused sand pit off the Common and sold, house to house, little wooden punnets of primroses, or violets, which Mother never bought as we could wander down the lane and get our own. She did however buy their clothes pegs made of white holly wood and bound round near the top with a thin band of tin cut from discarded food tins and secured with a tack. They were remarkably efficient.

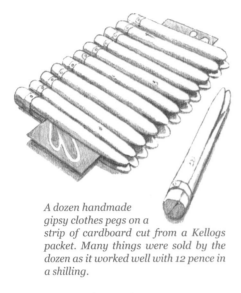

A dozen handmade gipsy clothes pegs on a strip of cardboard cut from a Kellogs packet. Many things were sold by the dozen as it worked well with 12 pence in a shilling.

We were always advised not to go near the gipsies temporary camps with their brightly coloured, horse-drawn caravans, each different, often designed and built by the owner. They varied between being not much more than a shed mounted on a flatbed trailer to the ultimate in coach building. Rightly or wrongly people believed they were not above stealing children. Whether there had ever been any justification for this I can't say, but I do remember a case in the newspapers about that time when a woman complained she had been cursed by a gipsy. Shortly after that there was talk of a law to be passed making it an offence to put a curse on anybody, so clearly there were people who believed a curse could work.

Rationing

Food rationing started on 8th January 1940. This was necessary because much of the country's food was imported. Shipping was in great danger from enemy submarines so it was important to keep imports restricted to essential supplies, materials which would aid the war effort. The weekly supply of rationed food per person was as follows as long as supplies arrived in your area. This could not be guaranteed because of the bombing and breakdown in services.

Meat to the value of 1 shilling and 2 pence *About 1 lb 3 oz. (Offal and sausages were not rationed, but one rarely saw a sausage.*
1 oz/28 gms Cheese
2 ozs/55 gms of the following: Butter, margerine, fat or lard, tea and jam
3 ozs/84 gms Sweets and sugar (This varied)
4 ozs/112 gms Bacon or ham
1 Egg
2 lb/900 gms Onions (only from 1942-44)
3 pints Milk
There were also points: 16 per month for tinned or dried food.
The price of food was strictly controlled by the Government.

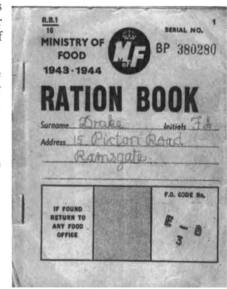

The mass production of chicken so prevalent now, did not exist at the time. It was a rare treat during wartime and the chicken spent rather happier lives in the farmyard eating grain and worms. In consequence not many reached the pot before their laying days were over so the birds were considerably tougher than is now the case. They required long slow cooking to be properly enjoyed but had the benefit of much more flavour than the present battery bred variety. Pork was also in short supply and we rarely had it. When we did we called it chicken. Same colour and we had anyway forgotten the taste of chicken. I do not know the reason for our shortage of pork. Probably little of it or perhaps it was the shortage of suitable food for pigs. They used to be fed swill; boiled up waste food of almost any sort including their own still-born piglets. Once the war started there was very little food waste for pigs or anybody else.

Our neighbour, Mrs Chandler, was very lucky, she had a large cat called Bunny because it quite frequently laid a rabbit on the doorstep when it returned from its nightly hunt. Ours only brought home shrews.

White bread now became grey bread as more of the normally discarded parts of the grain were retained to make supplies go further. Much of the wheat used in Britain had been imported from Canada but the huge danger to Atlantic shipping from German U-boats posed too great a risk except for essentials. In fact the extra roughage together with the rest of the wartime diet led to a healthier population. Nobody could eat too much and those on low incomes were entitled to the same diet as the rich. Bread was not rationed until after the war finished. We were much better off than many of our Euopeans neighbours.

A grocer removing coupons for a week's supply of tea, cheese, margarine, bacon and butter.

Rationing didn't stop with food. Anything that had to be imported, cotton, wood, fruit, all were either restricted or impossible to obtain. The Government issued plans for all furniture construction. They dictated the size, shape and finish of anything that was allowed to be made and it had to be made comparatively locally to reduce transport time and cost. It was called Utility Furniture, but although the design was rather minimallist the quality was quite good.

Clothing and bedding were subject to the same sort of control and were also strictly rationed. As with everything else, ration books with coupons for certain quantities were issued to everyone. These were cut out by the shop selling the product and had to be handed on by them to their suppliers in order to obtain the next shipment. No coupons, no goods. There were also points which could be spent on a variety of goods.These were items of personal choice and could be lavished on one item or on several products requiring fewer points. Newly marrieds got a slight concession in excess of others to start up their home.

For those who were too far from home for lunch, for travellers and those who could afford it, the local Councils set up British Restaurants in schools or public halls. On several ocassions, while staying with my grandfather in Ramsgate, I went for lunch with him at Ellington Girls' School, then empty of students who were all evacuated. The meals were cheap and not treated as part of ones ration, however restaurants were able to serve a person with either a meat or a fish course. Not both. Our meal cost one shilling and thru'pence i.e. 6p. I have read that those in London cost nine pence but the year may have been different or the meal subsidised. Privately owned restaurants also continued in business under similar restrictions, serving whatever they could get hold of at the time. Those living in the country with a garden fared better than those in to

This label was attached to all Utility products whether clothing or furniture as a guarantee of its basic quality.

Make do and mend

Darning, patching and knitting became the order of the evening or, when rarely women had time to sit down together. Worn sheets were cut down the centre and the unworn outer edges sewn together then cut across the middle so that the tops and bottoms formed the new middle. Old pullovers and cardigans were carefully unpicked, the wool being bundled into skeins and then washed and often re-dyed. When dry it became the lot of my brother, or myself, to sit with a skein stretched between our hands while my mother carefully rewound it into balls ready to make new garments. As we were growing the unpicked wool was seldom enough to make another pullover by itself so striped pullovers became the order of the day. Almost nothing got thrown away and I am still reluctant to part with old, comfortable clothes to the disgust of my wife, I arguing that they may come in handy when working in the garden of redecorating. During the war every hole or rip was painstakingly patched or darned. My socks often seemed more darn than original material.

Fortunately boys wore short trousers until they were about thirteen, though it seemed seldom we had a knee with no scab on it, our shorts only suffered attack from the back side. Women learnt how to knit socks using four steel needles with a point at each end. I have no idea how it was done but remember being told this system allowed them to change direction at the ankle. So much effort with the fine knitting involved. I thought of it this afternoon when my wife bought three pairs of socks in a bundle in the local £1 shop. When a hole appears they will go straight in the bin. We now live in a throw away society and value things much less; socks, mobile phones, televisions and computers costing vast sums of money are casually binned when a newer edition appears on the scene. Something seems wrong with our values. Perhaps we need a period of real hardship to bring us to a more intelligent use of our resources. On the other hand who needs to devote their life to the never ending drudgery of repair, cooking and washing when they can have a much more rewarding life in other fields.

Sewing machines like the one below, still in use in many homes, are a remnant of the days when things were not only made to look good. Built to last, many have been passed down five generations, given by successive mothers to their daughters when they themselves afforded to upgrade.

In common with others the village of Brindle in Lancashire formed a knitting circle to support and comfort the troops during the war years. Mothers, wives, aunts and grandmothers knitted, sewed and repaired for victory in response to the Government's call for everyone to "Do their Bit" for the war effort.

Women at War

Women worked in factories learning new skills, becoming milling machine operators, electricians, aircraft fitters, made munitions, organised the catering and much of the transport. They joined the Forces and took over jobs formerly done by men, who were badly needed in other fields. They played a vital part in plotting enemy aircraft and guiding our fighters to meet them. They drove ambulances and learnt how to service them as did the Queen, then Princess Elizabeth, with her sister as teenagers. My aunt, a trained nanny, became a milling machine operator in an ammunitions factory. There was plenty of work for them nursing the sick and wounded. They changed from being house-bound into financially independent people in charge of their lives and those of their family. The men were missing and women's roll in life changed, probably for ever.

The picture on the previous page illustrates a farm during the war. The farmer's wife on top of the stack is loading the threshing machine with the help of three Land Army girls and a man too old for military service.

The threshed straw dropped from the far end of the Ransomes threshing machine was then dumped onto a conveyor to build a straw stack to be used as bedding and roughage for cattle during the winter. The traction engine in the foreground was a fairground machine before the hostilities began but has been co-opted to provide the drive for the thresher. Most farm traction engines were black.

The chicken ensured that seed dropped from the corn did not go to waste.

The flywheel on the traction engine turned in one direction, but could turn the machine at the other end of the belt either way by using it as a simple elongated O or reversed by twisting it once into the form of a figure 8 as illustrated.

Threshing

The final part of the corn harvesting was of course the threshing. Few farms had their own threshing machine so used a contractor, who worked his way from client to client each year with a steam driven traction engine towing a threshing machine and sometimes also a hut on wheels in which he slept. Traction engines, certainly the most impressive of farm machines at that time, usually black, were sometimes painted green with red and gold trimmings for show ground use but could be co-opted for agricultural work during the war. Much like a steamroller without the rollers. Instead it had wheels suitable to give it grip on farmland. It sported a large flywheel which drove a long, thick canvas belt formed into a loop, the two ends joined by a metal buckle, the other end of the belt looped the drive wheel of the threshing machine making a thwack, thwack noise each time the buckle passed over the wheels. This was positioned next to a rick on top of which workers pitched the sheaves to a loader who fed them into the top of the thresher within which the seeds were removed from the chaff and stalk delivering a golden stream of grain into a sack at the back of the machine. Today's Health and Safety brigade would have had a field day on seeing this long completely unguarded belt arrangement.

Within a few years of the end of war the combined harvester came into common usage and traction engines disappeared from the workaday world. Farm machinery of the period was largely unguardable and often only used in difficult positions so that accidents were frequent. A farmer friend of my father had two of his sons killed. One fell off the back of a tractor to be crushed by the machine it was towing. The other was electrocuted while using portable sheep shearing equipment and accidentally cut a live cable while struggling with an animal. It was not uncommon to have tractors roll over on difficult terrain or by driving into a ditch in a heavily snow covered road or track. Another hazardous job even today is using a chain saw. A fallen tree appears to be a safe object lying static on the ground but branches bent from their normal angle can, when cut, spring violently, throwing the saw back at the user with disastrous results.

The village street

It was on the way down the hill from Lamberhurst Common to the village I one day saw my first artist sat on what is now a concrete bench seat. He was painting a watercolour of the cottages and Methodist Chapel (now converted to a house), where each Sunday, I sat with my mother and admired the sparkle of her engagement ring by holding her hand very close to my eye to pass away the sermon which I found less

A Bren gun carrier. A track driven transport vehicle with a Bren gun or other weapon mounted on it.

than fascinating. The artist had introduced into his picture a sports car painted maroon. I found this ridiculous as firstly, I had never seen a car of that colour, and there was seldom a car in the village as petrol was severely rationed. We were much more likely to see an army lorry or a bren-gun carrier. Just after the bench, on the same side but set well back from the road was a house built of cob, thick earthen walls. It has gone now, I suppose due to lack of a preservation order in the chaos of the post-war years. Rather sad as I know of no other in Kent.

Further down on the left-hand side was the entrance to a house which we called the colonel's house. It was here that we were issued with our gas masks. I was jealous of my younger brother's Micky Mouse mask while I had to have the standard version. These were supposed to be carried at all times in case of a gas attack. Mustard gas had been extensively used by the German's during the 1914-18 war. The masks were a bit claustrophobic and the celluloid window steamed up very easily. Everyone was also issued with an Identity Card for the war period, adults to carry one at all times, but as far as I recollect, children only needed theirs when travelling.

Lower down was the shop of Mr Wood, the cobbler. Part of his window was below the current street level. I used to stop to watch him sometimes, his mouth full of small nails as he fastened a new sole to a shoe. His son Brian was in my class. After that terrace came the baker, opposite was the sweet shop and then a hairdresser on the junction with the Hastings road. Just round the bend was Redman's garage from which my mother had to lug the paraffin can and our radio's glass accumulator each week after a fill up and recharging. Opposite stands the ancient Chequers Inn.

This view of the road outside the Chequers Inn in the centre of Lamberhurst was typical of village roads throughout the war years. With no vehicles in sight, games played in the gutter presented no danger to children. With the recently opened by-pass the village has a partial return to this peaceful state.

The centre of the village is traversed by the River Tees, a small stream, passing under the bridge. There was access down to the water on the lefthand side of this view and my school friend Basil and I clambered down to it one day to each steal a coot's egg. This was not a crime during that epoch and most boys had a collection and knowledge of birds' eggs and habitats. On one occasion the river flooded and we were unable to get to school. I am sure we were desperately disappointed. From here the road climbs towards the school. On the left, a terrace of cottages, the last of which housed Mrs Roberts, a widow leftover from the Victorian era who still wore a full length black crinoline dress. She was also a Sunday School teacher and we liked her very much. Then came Reeves the grocers with a collection of brass wire rabbit snares hanging outside the door to weather down their brassy colour and intended to trap people a ration free meal.

The Blacksmith and Wheelwright

Immediately before the school, and now built on, was the wheelwright's yard. They may well have also been builders, I cannot remember. It was the wheelwright that I found so fascinating. A cart wheel is a very interesting construction being slightly saucer shaped with the rim of the saucer towards the outside, not a flat thing like a wheelbarrow wheel. As a horse moves his body swings slightly from side to side obliging the cart to also swing first one way then back again. In the case of a heavily loaded cart this puts a considerable thrust from the axle on the one opposite. The wheel's rim is formed from sections of wood and this pressure would force the spokes outwards. If the wheels were built flat this thrust could punch out the centre if it were not for the iron rim. Because of the rim the wheel's joints are compressed by this action, not destroyed.

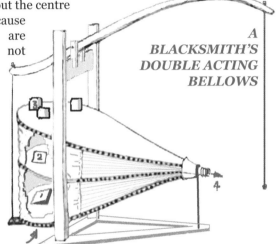

A BLACKSMITH'S DOUBLE ACTING BELLOWS

This wheelwright worked in conjunction with the next door blacksmith whose forge was attached to the school. On occasion, after school, I was allowed to work the double acting bellows for the black-smith.

The wheelwright would assemble a wheel or repair an existing one. It would then be laid on a special surface called a tyring plate and clamped there through is axle hole.The blacksmith would have previously walked round it pressing a measuring wheel against it to gauge the size of iron tyre.

The blacksmith used bellows similar to the above. Pulling on the cord lifted the lower section (1) forcing air through a flap into the upper chamber (2). Variable sized weights (3) on top of it controlled the force of the air out of the nozzle (4) which was connected by a tube to the fire and could create varying heats to mould or even melt iron.

Heated to bright red the iron tyre expanded about an eighth of an inch for each foot of the circumference. Too large and it would not hold the wheel together. Too tight and it would destroy the wheel as it shrank on cooling. An ancient wheelwright told me he could only get an accurate circumference going left-handed round the wheel. The other way always produced for him a slightly different measurement. Others preferred the opposite direction. The tyre would be heated to red hot in the forge then grasped by two, or three, men using tongs and hastily carried across the tyring table were it was lowered around the wheel and hammered into position. In its expanded state it would just fit on and start to shrink whereupon the wood would start smoking and a ring of flames start around the rim. The workmen would then pour water all around the rim, shrinking it in a cloud of steam to pull all the joints tight. It was a quite dramatic sight and a relief to all when finished without becoming distorted.

You may have seen horses pulling rubber tyred carts at country fairs and perhaps supposed that noise of horse traffic was a pleasant clip-clop-clip-clop. Not at all. Four feet diameter iron shod wheels make a fair amount of noise on flat modern roads. On the uneven gritted roads of my youth rather more a bumping rumble on the flat. Down hill with a laden cart a horse could be pushed over over

70

so a wooden shoed brake could be applied. As this was not very efficient with a heavy load the driver would slip a steel skid like a small sledge under the back wheels. The wheels ran into them and tobogganed down the slope to a screeching grinding noise.

When I was about sixteen I spent the Kent Week Regatta sailing in Whitstable. Having successfully destroyed a vital piece of equipment on the boat I had been sailing and waiting for its repair I found myself watching a local blacksmith plying his trade in a smithy on the waterfront. He had been a smith making, or repairing, fittings for the local oyster boats and Thames barges. With their gradual demise he had switched to making decorative ironwork and was constructing a garden gate with a decoration of acorns and oak leaves; very fine, easy work he made of it. On my return home at the end of the week I rushed to buy a length of iron from the local metal stockist and stuck it on the gas ring to heat up. Then I beat it to death for some time before realising that crafts which look so easy to the uninitiated are in fact the result of years and years of careful training and practice. Much of the ironwork sold now is shoddy, machine stamped work which is then welded together. Not the same delicacy or crispness as the hand-made product of a craftsman.

It would be very wrong to think that blacksmiths were just occupied with shoeing horses and repairing wheels. Many were extremely good engineers, had a lathe and could repair machinery, or fabricate new parts of machines when necessary. As transport turned more and more to motors many smithies became garages and the smith a mechanic who would repair a vehicle, and I mean repair. For the most part garages do not now repair; they exchange the broken bit with a replacement item. Hardly the same thing as skilfully fashioning a bit, but frequently the cheaper option in today's world.

Haymaking

On the farm behind us cutting and turning the hay in the 1940s was done by tractor. I had been allowed to watch so when the last of it had been pitch forked onto the horse drawn haywain I was delighted to be chucked up on top for a jerky, bouncy ride. It was then I found out that the husks, dust, pollen and the heat of a fine sunny day result in very scratchy, itchy clothing. The loose hay had to be stacked carefully, leaving ventilation spaces within the haystack to ensure there was no build up of heat caused by residual damp in the grass. Finally the top would be thatched. Without ventilation the humidity and following decomposition would create fire damp; heat that could produce spontaneous combustion. There were cases of this during our stay in the area and one of the resulting fires wiped out the entire rickyard and damaged surrounding buildings. The hay compacted under its own weight and during the winter months was sliced out in chunks to feed the horses, cattle and sheep.

Present day hay is mostly grown with the use of fertiliser and confined to seeds producing the maximum growth in the animals. This no doubt is best for the farmer but my own experience is with horses who, given the choice between that hay or mixed hay from meadow grass, will plump without hesitation for the latter with its mixture of plants and smells. Whether cattle and sheep would choose likewise I do not know, but I can tell you that the village children around us in France disliked it immediately when the cows providing our unpasteurised milk changed from grass feed to silage.

Hay stacks
Stacks like this have disappeared in Britain and most Western countries. From the 60s, after being cut and dried, hay was solidly compressed into rectangular, hand portable bales for storage in a barn. Rising labour costs have forced farmers to mechanise much more. The present system is to make round bales of up to a ton weight. Silage is the method of storing damp product such as grass or flaked maize direct from the field into clamps, airtight plastic containers, or silos, where it ferments and is used as a food supplement for cattle and sheep.

72

The next important part of the agricultural year for us was fruit picking, that is soft fruit, strawberries, raspberries and red or white currants. Opposite our home was a large strawberry field and the first year we were there we were allowed to go in and pick what we wanted. The following year the Ministry of Food, or Agriculture, or some other decided that the total output must go to a jam factory. By then farmers were being told what they could, or could not grow and what was to happen to it afterwards. In fact, after the crop had been collected the field was opened up and we were allowed to pick the late ripening fruit, so were much luckier than folk living in towns.

Hop picking

The school year had been divided up to suit the agricultural seasons starting from the Hop Picking holiday so named because it coincided with the time we were invaded by many Londoners and others who took a working holiday in the hop gardens of Kent and Sussex each year.

A farm worker on stilts repairing the trellis of wires which supported the hop bines. Strings from the centres of the wires were attached to the hooks at the base of each pole to form vaulted corridors for the vines.

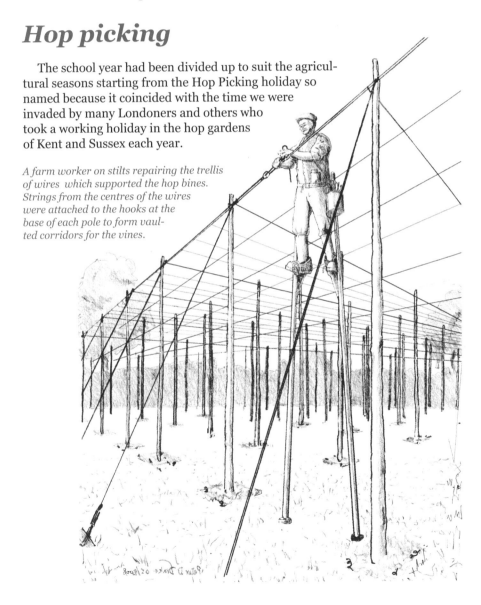

Hops are an important ingredient in the production of beer as they make it bitter to counteract the sweetness of another ingredient, malt. They also affect the flavour and smell. The fields in which hops are grown are called hop gardens. Grown in Kent, Sussex, Hampshire, Herefordshire, Warwickshire, Wiltshire and Worcestershire, hops are a climbing plant and the gardens had rows of poles between four and five metres high, joined by a criss-cross of wires. There were often poles stood in barrels of a black preservative outside oast houses, ready as replacements where necessary. Strings from above to four hooks anchored in the ground in a square at the foot of each pole supported the growing hop bine which was planted within it.

These hopper's huts in Goudhurst, Kent, used to house five families for their annual working holiday and represented the better end of such housing. Others were packed into barns with virtually no privicy. It is difficult to imagine in these days of international holidays, that country air and rough accommodation once gave so much fun and laughter as well as work and discomfort to a quarter of a million people each year.

Twice a year thousands of acres of hop garden needed a temporary workforce. As the bines started to grow the tendrils had to be "twisled" onto the strings to start their upward journey, and again for picking from the second half of August through into mid September. Around 250,000 casual workers, up to 80,000 in Kent alone, including vast numbers of people from East London used to travel on "Hoppers' Specials", trains which transported them to the country after rush hour. Collected at the station by horse and cart, lorries and on flat farm trailers pulled by tractors, they were carried to the various farms where they joined the army of other itinerant farm workers and gypsies to spend a working holiday in cramped brick huts, in barns with a only a tarpaulin or blanket between families, or in tents.

Hops on the bine

74

A HOP PICKING WORKING HOLIDAY

Hop growing in Britain is reputed to have been introduced from Holland and started near Canterbury, Kent, in 1520. As the taste for bitter beer instead of plain ale spread, so did the area producing hops. A century and a half later fourteen counties were producing hops, a third of the total being in Kent. Because of the enormous workforce needed, growing became largely restricted to the proximity of industrial areas with large populations, around London, South Wales and the West Midlands.

The industry has had its ups and downs. It grew to a maximum of 77,000 acres by 1878. After this the quantity declined slowly due to the import of cheaper product from abroad. By the early 1900s it was down to 32,000 acres and by 2003 just 3,000 acres. With post-war full employment getting pickers became difficult, from 1948 and through the 50s farmers all over England gradually changed over to mechanical picking and 400 years of agricultural life died except for a few acres by traditionalist farmers.

For many of the children this was their first glimpse of life outside the city. Families cooked outside on open fires; it was like a gypsy camp and some of them were quite rough. I know one pub on the village hill had a notice outside, "No gypsies or hop pickers", which I thought a bit rude to the visitors. My recollection is that they were mainly female, well built grandmas with their daughters or daughters–in–law and children but of course it was wartime so most of the men were otherwise occupied.

The bines were pulled down by the farm workers and hand picked into sacking bins set on a trestle arrangement. After measuring, the workers received payment for the number of bushel picked. *(A bushel is a bulk measure of about 35 litres, see p87).* The measurer making sure that there were no leaves in the bin. All this is now done by clever machinery.

After picking they were carted to the oast house where they were dried on the first floor of the old square, or later round kilns. This had a slatted floor covered with horse hair mats or hessian through which the heat of the burning wood, charcoal or anthracite could permiate to gently dry the hops for about eight hours without cooking them. The tall cowl on top of the kiln pivotted like a weather vane to turn its open side away from the wind and draw the hot air up from the fire. The hops were then raked into the area above the barn to cool before being packed into pokes or pockets, *(very tall sacks holding about 168 pounds/76 kg)* and sent to market.

TYPICAL KENTISH OAST HOUSES

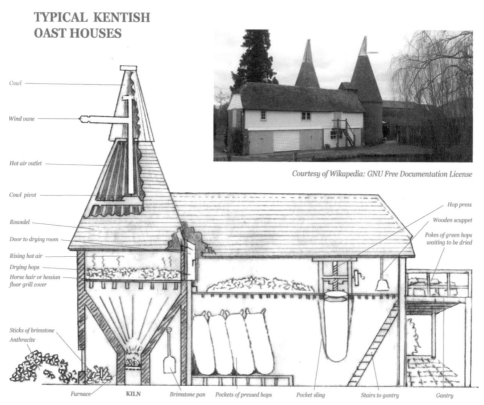

Courtesy of Wikapedia: GNU Free Documentation License

76

Infants School

I started school in the autumn of 1941 after the Hop Picking Holiday. The school was at the other end of the village, a walk of about a mile and a quarter, there being no buses in that direction. In fact we varied it by sometimes going down the hill and sometimes crossing the Common and passing through two fields and then the hop garden beside which were the small brick huts in which the pickers stayed. I was at first accompanied by an older girl, probably seven or eight-years-old. There was no fear of being snatched, or attacked at that time and quite young children were often unaccompanied. For my seventh birthday I was given a secondhand bike and travelled independently.

Lamberhurst village School with the old smithy to the left, now converted to a house. The school is interesting as the architecture is Huguenot with its typical Dutch gable ends. One of the charms of English villages is the mixture of building styles. With room to expand they have not needed to destroy the architectural heritage which tells so much of their history.

I enjoyed the small, Victorian, church owned infants' school. The classes were run by two middle-aged ladies, Miss Francis and Mrs Playfoot. We cut out pictures of vegetables and stuck them onto paper then wrote the names beside them. I still have my first writing and maths books. Writing, apart from the foregoing, was mostly copying verses of hymns that we had sung in the village church, visited crocodile fashion each week, or comments about the day. We noted one day that "Drake has been lazy".

I liked the church because it had silver grey wooden shingles instead of slates or tiles. I believe that is still the case. Perhaps my first interest in architecture. I have ever since found it a very attractive way to top off a building. We learnt our tables up to 12 x 12 by chanting them like a liturgy, also the basics of maths which at that time I enjoyed enormously. Basic Victorian education, much of the work done on a slate with a slate pencil and cleaned at the end of the lesson with a damp cloth. Whether this was an exigency of the war, because of the shortage of paper or simply the way it had always been I do not know. Certainly the exercise books I have preserved are normal exercise books cut in half horizontally, presumably for economy.

That was the year I learnt the truth about Father Christmas. I had for some time understood that fairies and gnomes did not exist. Now this blow! What other lies had been perpetrated on me? I remember thinking: "How old will I be when they tell me that God doesn't exist". I have to say that it never did happen, both my parents remained firm believers to their dying day but that Christmas marked the start of my path to doubt. It is mistake to suppose very young children just accept adult arguments.

School dinners were supplied in a building on the opposite side of the village street, we marched there in a crocodile. The smell as we neared it was of murdered vegetables; not just well cooked; cooked to extinction. From time to time I have smelt it again and am instantly transported back to those lunches. Remember that as there was no refrigerator we ate those vegetables that were harvested at that particular time of year.

A yoke

In winter swedes, turnips and carrots, in the summer we had lettuce and tomatoes. Later it was cabbage or Brussels sprouts, these cooked to a rather horrid brown colour. Meat was in very short supply and frequently seemed to be mostly gristle so must have presented quite a challenge to the cook. The dessert I recall was spotted dick, a very filling suet pudding with a sprinkling of currants, or sultanas, in it, topped with a rather revolting lumpy custard. Whatever, it did us no harm and these dinners helped to supplement our diet without reducing our rations. We were also entitled to a daily third of a pint of milk to ensure we had sufficient calcium in our diet. Milk was delivered daily to houses in the towns by milkmen who left it early in the morning on the doorstep. It came in glass, one pint bottles with a circular, waxed cardboard lid jammed in the top. This had a push-in centre so that one could hook a finger through it and pull it off. If people wished to change their order they just put a note in one of the empties and left them on the doorstep in the evening. The milkman did a second round later on Saturdays to collect payment. In the country things were different, there was another choice, milk did not have to be pasteurised and we could buy from the bailiff of a farm just off the east side of the Common. An elderly man, he carried two small churns suspended on a yoke across his shoulders and ladled it out into his customer's jugs. The school milk also came in a churn.

The school playground overlooks fields on one side, a lovely setting in which to grow up. I recall the names of several of my fellow students; Jimmy Haskell, Roger Marshall and Brian Wood. My best friend was Basil Kemp whose father worked on Ridge farm and lived in a cottage there. I recall birds nesting with him and being shown the nest of a bottle tit, (the Kentish name for a longtailed tit) with many eggs. We took one each. The school's headmaster was a Mr Noakes who lived in the section of the school building adjoining the smithy and in my memory he was a pleasant man, who wore a mustard coloured tweed suit. I feared the teacher we would have for the following year, we called her "Goosey", she was reputed to be a bit of a dragon. As luck would have it we quit Lamberhurst before that happened. That was 1944, the year school leaving age was increased from fourteen to fifteen years of age.

Early in my time there we had a visit from the village policeman. He produced a large poster illustrating a selection of pretty brooches, fountain pens and so on. We were told that should we find any of these types of thing we must not touch them, just call the police or a soldier. The Germans were dropping them as they flew over the country and they would explode if touched. So far as I know nobody in the school ever found one, but the memory of that visit remains with me and others of my generation to whom I have mentioned it. As time went on we got to know the distinctive sound of enemy aircraft, quite unlike our own, also to learn the names of the different types, both friend and foe.

Other publicity of the time warned against loose talk. Do not mention convoys of army vehicles, or troop movements, to other people. Who knew whether a listener was a German spy and what use they could have made of the information.

Boys' toys, games and treasures

With the war toys changed from Hornby trains and cars to guns, model aircraft and tanks, mostly home-made from wood as factories now had to make armaments. The treasures that filled our pockets were army hat and shoulder badges. Toys disappeared from the shops. On a visit I remember finding only a kazoo suitable for my age group. Some old traditions cling on, but the ancient game of marbles has largely fallen victim to the traffic. Generations of boys have played it on the roadside and in my village childhood there was seldom need to get out of the way of cars. With the advent of war there was a bonus of occasional free marbles. Tank ball bearings, which for some unexplained reason were sometimes found by the roadside after a military convoy had passed through the village, counted for ten in a game of marbles played in the gutter on the way home. A red glass one, called a "ruby" or a "blood alley" was worth six of any other. Bits of rubber from tank wheels were hoarded as swappable treasure, don't ask me why, it was completely useless. Something else to stuff in our pockets or our ever present gas mask cases.

CARELESS TALK COSTS LIVES

A wartime poster reminding people that there may be Nazi sympathisers passing information to our enemy.

Prior to the war cigarette manufacturers included a card in each packet of ten cigarettes, two in a packet of twenty. Each card was one of a set, usually of twenty-five or fifty, depicting anything from famous footballers to fighter aircraft or wild birds. Children collected them, swopping spares with friends to try to get a full set. Spares were used to play a game called fag cards. Two or more players would sit on the ground about five feet from a wall and flick a card towards it in turn. The game was to land a card on top of one already down, you then took all the cards that lay on the floor. With the war economies these cards were discontinued so we collected the outside of cigarette packets as fag cards and played with them instead. As I recall, top value were Craven A, a bright red packet followed by any other.

Games like this had seasons, one minute everyone was playing fag cards then conkers would arrive and we were all trying to get the hardest conker. Some soaked them in vinegar and baked them. Some dried them over a period. Each had his own theory on how to get a winner. The conker was then threaded onto a leather bootlace or a piece of strong string long enough to keep your fingers well away from the conker and avoid an opponent accidentally whacking your fingers while trying to strike your conker hard enough to break it with his own. Each win added a point to your score so a conker became a twoer, a threer, a fourer and so on. If you managed to break the oppositions conker its score could be added to that of your own so if your fourer broke a tenner some agued it became a fourteener.

The next month marbles could be back in fashion, then five-stones, a game where the players throw five small stone cubes in the air and try to catch them on the back of their hand, those falling on the floor have to be picked with the same hand without dropping any of those already on its back. There were further complications of difficulty as the game continued.

Fag cards, more correctly called cigarette cards, had further details of the picture subject on their back.

Another craze was hoops. A ring of iron of about 7mm diameter rod formed into a circle approximately the height of a bicycle wheel, which we hit with a stick as we walked or ran along the road trying not to let it fall over. Of course there were always chasing games like tag. The person being chased was called "It" or "He".

To select who should be "It" we said a rhyme, pointing at each person in turn. The person pointed to at the last word became "It". There were a number of similar rhymes.

Eeni meeni maka raka
Ere I dominaca
Chika paka lolly cracker
Om pom push.

Girls games

Girls had their own games but as I never had a sister I can only tell you what I saw. Of their treasures during the war I saw nothing except that dolls and teddy bears were favourites. Where games were concerned, they chased one another as the boys did and played hopscotch, which I see has survived to the present day although there was a recent crazy prosecution of a child for defacing the public footpath with chalk in order to play it. Apparently as the police officer hadn't got sufficient thieves into his net he was looking for an easier way to keep up his success rate.

Skipping was very popular, sometimes with long ropes so that several girls skipped at the same time. They had names for the various ways of skipping, with the rope going forwards or backwards, or very fast so the rope passed under them twice with only one jump or for variety hopping on alternate legs.

There were old games in a circle. One I remember was called "In and out the dusty bluebells" in which the girls formed a circle holding hands with their arms in the air to form arches. The girl called "It" wove in and out of the circle under the raised arms while the group sang the first verse.

1st verse:
In and out the dusty blue bells,
In and out the dusty blue bells,
In and out the dusty blue bells,
I am your Master.

2nd verse:
Give a little pit-a-pat on her shoulder,
Give a little pit-a-pat on her shoulder,
Give a little pit-a-pat on her shoulder,
I am your Master.

At the end of the first verse wherever "It" was, she stood behind the nearest girl tapping her on the shoulder as she alone sang the second verse, at the end of which that girl went behind her, then, holding her waist, they would start weaving in and out again, all repeating the song until the chain left insufficient girls to make a circle.

Skating was popular with both sexes after the war when they could be manufactured again. Unlike rollerblades of the present, the four wheels were of steel and would not work properly on grit or rough surfaces so we were restricted to flat paving, tarmac or a rink. The skates clipped onto the welt of the shoes toe and strapped across the instep. The length was adjustable.

School holidays and celebrations

On May Day (May 1st) a pole was erected in the playground and the girls danced round it holding coloured ribbons and weaving in and out of one another to wrap the pole in a colourful pattern. When the pole was completely wrapped they reversed their direction to unwind it again. Not a simple feat as an error by one girl would have caused complete confusion. I recall this event only once during the war years. It continues in a few villages to this day.

Dancing around a Maypole at Barwick-in-Elmet, Yorkshire. Courtesy of the Barwick Maypole Trust. "Maypole Dancing."

The summer holiday was called the Hop Picking Holiday but certainly picking the hops was not always completed during that holiday period as I recall once passing through a busy hop garden after the return to school. The next break, apart from half-term, was at Christmas then Easter and May Day followed by Fruit Picking which was designed to coincide with the strawberry and raspberry harvesting, thereby allowing children to help parents pick the fruit. There were also Bank and religious holidays like Ascension Day and Whitsun. Not holidays, but regarded as special days to celebrate England, were St George's Day (23rd April) and 19th May to celebrate King Charles II's restoration to the throne and his hiding in an oak while being hunted by Cromwell's troops. For that day we all wore an oak leaf to school.

Oak leaves and an acorn

82

Money

The old Imperial coinage was made up of pounds, shillings and pence, halfpence and farthings. Four farthings or two ha'pennies making one penny. Twelve pence made a shilling and twenty shillings or two hundred and forty pence made one pound. Coins were the copper farthing, ha'penny and penny, thru'penny pieces (three pence) a twelve sided brass coloured coin that had largely superceeded the older silver "joey" as it was called, though it was still in production until 1941. Then came the silver sixpence known as a tanner, followed by the shilling, usually referred to as a"bob", a florin or two bob bit and the half crown (two shillings and six pence) commonly called half a dollar as that was roughly its value against the American currency. Further up the scale was the crown which was really a collectors item, not in general circulation. Higher denominations came in paper money, ten shillings, then one, five and ten pound notes. The last two known respectively as a fiver and a tenner. By 1950 five pounds represented a week's wages for many people and was much more than I earned per week until 1956 by which time I had been apprenticed for four years and reached the grand old age of twenty. At the start of it I had only received £1 :7s : 6d per week. £1.35p in our present currency.

Prices were written £ : s : d. For instance £17 : 13s : 8d. Seventeen pounds, thirteen shillings and eight pence. The "d" dated back to the Roman occupation of our country and stood for dinarius. The farthing, ha'penny and three farthings were added after the pence column as fractions of a penny. None of this made maths any easier. Take a nice simple example. Three men, having eaten at an hotel are dividing the above example bill between them. The pounds are divided by three, the remainder multiplied by 20 is added to the shillings column, the remainder of that multiplied by 12 then added to the pence column. Still one column to go. You think life is complicated nowadays? And we had no pocket calculator!

All coins carried the king or queen's head on the other side like this example bearing that of the young Queen Victoria. This coin is a Groat. Four pence. It was discontinued in 1856. I found one in my change during the 1956. Slightly thicker than a silver threepenny bit, but the same diameter, it had survived unnoticed as small change for about ninety years. The silver "Joeys" were often put into the Christmas pudding when I was young for us children to find and add to the excitement of the day. Britain converted to decimal currency on 15 February 1971.

Farthing

Ha'penny

Penny

Silver "joey" and Thru'penny bit

Sixpence or "tanner"

Shilling or "bob"

Florin or "two bob bit"

Half-crown

83

DATES:

The issue of coins containing silver ceased in 1947. Thereafter these coins were made of cupronikel. This was because the cost of silver exceeded the face value of the coins.

Production of "Ship ha'pennies", so called because the reverse side carried an image of Drake's Golden Hind started in 1937 and finished as did production of the farthing in 1948. During the war children were asked to collect "Ship ha'pennies" to help the Navy. I was never told whether this was to buy comforts for the sailors or to build more ships.

British currency was decimalised on 15th February 1971.

Our tables were learnt by chanting them in class, over and over. Old fashioned teaching perhaps but never to be forgotten:

12 pence is one shilling
18 pence is one and sixpence
24 pence is two shillings
30 pence is two and sixpence
36 pence is three shillings
40 pence is three and fourpence
48 pence is four shillings
50 pence is four and tu'pence
60 pence is five shillings
66 pence is five and six pence
72 pence is six shillings

80 pence is six and eight pence
84 pence is seven shillings
90 pence is seven and sixpence
96 pence is eight shillings
100 pence is eight and fourpence
108 pence is nine shillings
112 pence is nine and fourpence
120 pence is ten shillings
130 pence is ten and ten pence
132 pence is eleven shillings
140 pence is eleven and eight pence
144 pence is twelve shillings

Thank goodness we stopped at this point, but all our times tables were learnt up to 12 times whatever, because twelve was a basic unit both in money and measurement. Doubtless having to learn the above aided our flexibility when doing other calculations. Because our monetary calculations were based on 12d it made sense to buy things in dozens rather than tens. Materials, pipe, rope, curtain rail etc. were sold by the foot, 12 inches. Eggs for instance came in dozens or half dozens as did very many other items. We sold eggs in boxes of 30 dozen to bakers. There was also a "Baker's dozen", thirteen! If you bought a dozen buns you got one free.

Speaking of coinage I should mention a major difference with that of today. Before metrification our coins were frequently old. I mean really old. In my youth it was quite common to find you were spending coins that had been in use for almost a hundred years with the head of a young Queen Victoria on it worn almost flat in places from jingling with its mates in vast numbers of pockets. Money that had been spent countless times before the birth of my grandfather, minted almost fifty years before the birth of the motor car. Pennies that had once been worth more when minted than the silver sixpences or shillings had by the end of their lives. When the silver content of coins exceeded their face value it did not escape the notice of the Mint who then used cupronickel to save money. The money we carry now has almost no metallic scrap value, the coins might just as well be plastic counters except that they would be more easily counterfeited.

In the 40s and 50s comparatively few people had a bank account. Those who did had no need of a security number. If the bank trusted one enough to open an account, that was sufficient guarantee of their customer's honesty. As more and more companies decided to pay their staff monthly instead of weekly as had been the custom, so did the number of bounced and/or forged cheques requiring more protection for both banks and the public at large. Up till then all transactions were recorded on paper. Bank guarantee cards were issued, followed in 1966 by Barclaycards with hole-in-the wall cashpoints the following year.

A pre-decimalisation cash register

A Post Office savings book

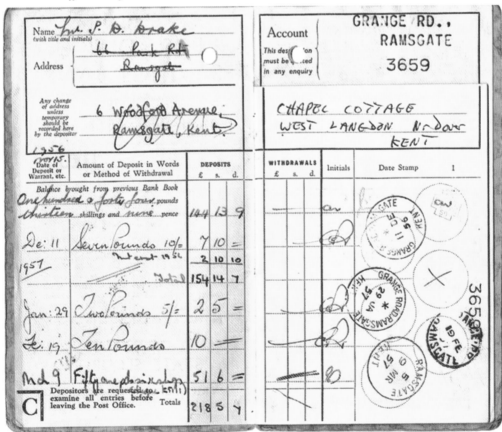

At the present time we are seeing the end of metallic money and moving fast towards a cashless society. Plastic has come into is own with credit cards, hole-in-the-wall machines, electronic transfers of money by Swift, internet banking etc. The French Government is now trying to persuade its citizens to use a Moneo card, like a debit card which can be charged up at any cash point direct from one's bank account. It is to be used at no cost for small payments such as a coffee, snacks etc., where the supplier is unwilling to accept a normal card payment on which he would be obliged to pay commission. Likewise a payment may be made by a card holder by inserting his card into the recipient's card holder. Voila! No need for cash. No black economy. All transactions of money electronically traceable. Advertising in the bank says, and I translate freely, "To all account holders! Get your free Moneo Card now". Amazingly the uptake has not been a tremendous success. I will not be surprised if ever more than 50% of the population have the card, the Government announce the end of coinage, obliging the rest of the population to join. Just imagine a country with no black economy, taxation could probably fall by ten percent or more to the benefit of the population.

Measurement

British coinage and measures have partly been in use from the time of the Romans, and brought to us again from Normandy in 1066AD. Conversion to the Napoleonic metric system was ignored in the late 1700s, probably because it was from France with whom we were then at war. I have had occasion to survey a number of pre-Napoleonic houses in France and found that they were more conveniently measured using my Imperial tape measure. Window reveals often 4' 0" apart, doors commonly thirty one and a half inches wide as are many Victorian interior doors. Rooms measuring a certain number of feet by a certain number of feet, measurements that do not fit neatly into the metric system. A builder is unlikely to build a room twelve feet eight and a quarter inches wide. He would either go for twelve feet, twelve feet six inches or thirteen feet. It's easier. Likewise for the French prior to the introduction of metric measure. Following the revolution of 1789 rooms were likely to be to the nearest ten centimetres.

In the distant past accurate measurement was largely unnecessary and it was convenient to have a system that everyone carried with them. Feet being commonly attached to the bulk of surveyors, it was logical to use them. We still use hands to measure the height of horses. Of course their 4" width varies slightly with the owner but it is near enough to give a fairly accurate picture. The French still stick to the "pouce" (thumb) when referring to bicycle wheel sizes; this is actually the British inch. In Britain we now have a real hotch-potch, part Imperial and part metric measure.

Distance			Weight			Volume		
1 inch	=	2.5 cm approx	1 ounce	=	28.3 gms	1 gill *(liquid)*	=	0.142 ltr
1 foot	=	30.5 cm	1 pound	=	453.5 gms	1 pint	=	0.568 ,,
1 yard	=	91.4 cm	1 stone	=	6.3kg	1 quart	=	1.136 ,,
1 furlong	=	201.17m	1 hundredweight	=	50.8 kg	1 gallon	=	4.546 ,,
1 mile	=	1.61 kilometres	1 ton	=	1,016 kg	1 bushel *(dry)*	=	35 ,,

Volume

There was quite a business manufacturing containers for soft fruit which now arrives in weighed, lidded plastic trays. They were made of poplar wood strips, cut so thin it could be woven, tapered towards the base for easy stacking. They came in two shapes; a square punnet for small quantities or a chip, oblong, with a metal handle across the mid point that could swivel aside for stacking. Chips were about 30cm long. They were not weighed, just filled to the top. Pecks and bushels were two other dry measures of volume. A peck container was one that could hold the equivalent bulk of 8 quarts of liquid and a bushel equalled 4 pecks. The weight of either varied as it depended on whether the goods were sprouts, or potatoes, or oats.

A bushel basket of hops and a chip of strawberries.

Weight

Common weights were as follows:

The ounce, commonly marked oz. Example 6ozs.
16 ounces made one pound (written lb)
14 pounds equalled 1 stone (st)
  2 stone was called a quarter (qtr)
  8 stone or 4 quarters equalled 1 hundredweight (cwt)
20 hundredweight or 2,240 pounds made 1 ton (T)

Salter scales bought by my mother in 1934 and used almost daily for the next fifty odd years. No battery, nothing to go wrong but a trifle heavy.

Above: Part of a stocktaking entry showing the amount of margarine held at three depots. All book-keeping records were hand written. Although in this case the writer has not used the columns to line up his work, ledgers were ruled to suit the customers requirements. This was done by the bookbinder, not the printer, using a machine with very fine knibs, set at whatever spacing the client required.

Fluids

Liquid measure was equally irregular:
>   4 gills made a pint
>   2 pints made a quart
>   4 quarts to the gallon

This is a one pint milk bottle of the shape used in the 1940s with its waxed cardboard top which was just pressed in. The centre has a part perforation, just push it in with your finger and hook out the lid. Later these were replaced by foil tops, but had the disadvantage that tits learnt to peck a hole in them for a free drink.

Land

Distance was measured in inches, feet, yards, rods/poles/perches, chains, furlongs and miles.

The inch, abbreviated as in. or ” for example 10”
>   12 inches = 1 foot or ft. or ’ for example 10’
>   3 feet = 1 yard
>   5 yds 1 ft 6ins = 1 rod/pole/perch (name varies)
>   4 rods = 1 chain or 22 yards (the length between the stumps for cricket.)

Area

Land area in Britain was, and still is at the time of writing, measured in acres.
>   1   Acre=4,840 sq yds
> *Or* 1 furlong x 10 chains

I understand the name furlong was arrived at because one furrow was as far as the normal 8 bullock plough could be pulled in heavy soil without giving a rest to the animals i.e. a furrow long.

Sea and others

Distance at sea is measured in fathoms (6 feet), chains (22 yards, the standard length of a cricket pitch), cables (100 fathoms) and nautical miles (basically 10 cables) and has no relationship with land miles.

There are, or were, many other curious measures in common usage. In the letterpress printing business for instance there are the point and the em.
12 points = 1 em and 6 ems= 1 inch

As you will now see, the whole measurement system evolved by series of accidents over hundreds of years. Local custom in one area would, if convenient, spread to the next and gradually crept into common usage. It is sad to witness the end of these quaint, historic evolutions, but I wish the metric system had been in use when I was at school. I might have been rather better at maths, a subject which completely floored me at grammar school.

Roads and their maintenance

It is a common misconception that in the past everyone travelled on horseback, or in a coach. In fact many rarely left their village and when they did it was, as my grandmother put it, "On Shanks's pony". Walking. With the arrival of cars it was again the comparatively well to do who had one. After their invention the common alternative was the bicycle, never allowed on the footpath. Just as well, travel presented considerable problems during the war years. Posters everywhere asked: "Is your journey really necessary?" Police, postmen, delivery boys and workmen all used their feet or bicycles. At seven years old I received my first bike to make the mile-and-a-quarter ride to school.

Nowadays the roads and lanes are cleaned by lorries, the hedges cut by tractors, the ditches maintained by mechanical diggers. One or two maintenance men can cover a vast area. The years immediately preceeding the war were seeing the start of modern roads and a few stretches of concrete road had been constructed. There were no motorways and a car journey from Ramsgate to London was a good four hours with very heavy congestion on the sections through the Medway towns. Incidentally these new, pre-war sections of bright concrete road were hurriedly tarred and gritted when it was realised they made useful navigation aids to enemy aircraft. The first major section of motorway in Britain, 193 miles of the M1, was not opened until 1959.

Hedging and ditching, as we called the maintenance of the hedgerows and ditches, was the work of the roadman. He would arrive on his bike, or on foot, and poke a forked stick into the verge, hang on it his coat, gas mask and satchel containing a bottle of cold tea, lunch tin and his sharpening stone. He would then work his way steadily down the road using a sickle or billhook and a hook with which to pull awkward branches towards him. The hook would have been cut from a hazel bush, about four feet long with a branch growing up at about forty-five degrees at the bottom end. Any other branches would be cleaned off then the stick reversed

Do not confuse bikes of that era with those of today. They were heavy steel frames designed to last a lifetime. Rod brakes instead of cable and no gears. The small square bracket just below the handlebars was for the light which could be of the new battery powered type or an acetylene gas lamp as in this picture. The gas was produced by water dripping on to acetylene the flow of water controlled by the tap on top.

Wartime lamps had to have a deflector to minimise the amount of light shown as it was thought this could attract enemy aircraft.

so that he held what had been the top end. An instant, no cost council tool. On other occasions he might have a spade, or scythe, to clean out the ditch or cut the verge. It was a matter of pride to make his stretch of the road at least as neat as the other road men. He would also be expected to take care not to chop off any oaks growing up through the hedge.

In my mind's eye I can see him now, going on sixty so too old for the forces though doubtless a member of the Home Guard, going bald, wearing a collarless shirt. Many shirts of the period had detachable collars fixed by a collar stud front and back, so that a collar could be replaced with a clean one without the need to wash the entire shirt. Over this he would wear a sleeveless waistcoat, his shirt sleeves rolled up above his elbows. His trousers from the same old suit as his waistcoat, its colour originally black, now somewhat faded like the muzzle of an elderly, once black dog. The ensemble finished by well worn heavily creased black leather boots. At lunch time he would make himself comfortable on the bank, or a fallen tree trunk and take out his battered lunch tin. Nothing would disturb him. Very few cars passed, with petrol rationing most people's cars were under cover awaiting the end of the war.

Most roads were macadamed, that is to say tarred and gritted. Built for horse transport. As cars seldom travelled at much more than forty-five miles an hour it was not necessary for them to be as smooth and flat as they are today. Every year or so a team of men arrived with lorries loaded with grit and a tanker full of tar with which to spray the road before throwing the grit over it in a sweeping motion with their shovels. This procession was follow by a steamroller. That was the interesting part for me. These great machines with the front of the boiler decorated with a cast iron or brass rampant horse and the word Invicta can still be seen at steam fairs on Bank holidays. Now they are treated with all the respect due to elderly ladies but they were much more impressive trundling up and down a newly gritted road with the water running over their great wheels to stop the tar sticking to them, steam discharging all around and the smell of the molten tar, oil and coal smoke. Only railway steam engines and traction engines were more interesting for me.

Public Notices

Public transport was reduced and the single decker bus that passed our gate going too and from Tunbridge Wells carried stickers on the window asking "Is Your Journey Really Necessary". Others exhorted us to "Dig for Victory" and "Waste Not Want Not", also to avoid various other wasteful sins suggested by the Squanderbug. This illustrated character bore a remarkable likeness to Hitler. Further advertisements implored women to knit socks for the troops overseas, or to cook carrots for their families, supposed to help us see in the dark. Remember there was no longer any street lighting in Britain.

BEWARE

HE WANTS TO KNOW YOUR UNIT'S NAME.
WHERE YOU'RE GOING. WHENCE YOU CAME.
EVEN ALONE OR IN A CROWD
NEVER MENTION THESE OUT LOUD.

Lunchtime for the "Hedging and Ditching" roadman.

AFTER THE RAID

ISSUED BY THE MINISTRY OF HOME SECURITY
PROVINCIAL EDITION   DECEMBER, 1940

AFTER THE RAID

WHEN YOU HAVE been in the front line and taken it extra hard the country wants to look after you. For you have suffered in the national interest as well as in your own in the fight against Hitler. If your home is damaged there is a great deal of help ready for you.

You will want to know where this help can be found and whom to ask about it. Here are some hints about how you stand. Remember, in reading them, that conditions are different in different areas and the services may not always be quite the same.

HAVE YOUR PLANS READY

YOU SHOULD TRY to make plans *now* to go and stay with friends or relations living near, but not too near, *in case your house is destroyed.* They should also arrange *now* to come to you if their house is knocked out.

If you have to go and stay with them until you can make more permanent arrangements the Government will pay them a lodging allowance of 5s. per week for each adult and 3s. for each child. Your host should enquire at the Town Hall or Council offices about this.

Find out now, in case of emergency, from the police or wardens where the offices are at which the local authority and the Assistance Board are doing their work for people who have been bombed.

1

FOOD AND SHELTER

IF YOU HAVE NOT been able to make arrangements with friends or relatives and have *nowhere to sleep and eat* after your house has been destroyed, the best thing to do is to go to an emergency *Rest Centre*. The wardens and policemen will tell you where this is. You will get food and shelter there until you can go home or make other arrangements. You will also find at the Rest Centre an officer whose job it is to help you with your problems. He will tell you how to get *clothes* if you've lost your own, *money* —if you are in need—a new ration book, a new identity card, a new gas mask, etc.

NEW HOMES FOR THE HOMELESS

A HOME WILL BE FOUND for you, if you cannot make your own arrangements. If you are still earning your normal wages you may have to pay rent.

If you can make arrangements to go and stay with friends or relatives, you will be given a free travel voucher if you cannot get to them without help. Enquire about this at the Rest Centre.

TRACING FRIENDS AND RELATIVES

TO KEEP IN TOUCH with your friends and relatives you should, if you find your own accommodation, send your new address to the Secretary, London Council of Social Service, 7, Bayley Street, Bedford Square, London, W.C.1. Of course, also tell your friends and relatives where you are.

2

Anyone who is homeless and has been provided with accommodation can be found through the Town Halls, the Council offices and the Citizens' Advice Bureaux, since records are kept.

If you have got sons or daughters in the Army, Navy, R.A.F., or the Auxiliary Services, they can find you, too, through their Commanding Officer, wherever you may be, whether you have gone to the country, are in hospital or are with friends.

FURNITURE AND OTHER BELONGINGS

(1) *If your income is below a certain amount* you can apply to the Assistance Board for :—
  (a) a grant to replace *essential furniture** and *essential* household articles ;
  (b) a grant to replace your clothes† or those of your family ;
  (c) a grant to replace *tools†* essential to your work.

You also have a claim for your other belongings, but these do not come under the Assistance Board's scheme, and you should make your claim on Form V.O.W.1.‡

(2) *If your income is above certain limits* you do not come under the Assistance Board's scheme and should make out a claim for all your belongings on Form V.O.W.1.‡

The time at which payment can be made for belongings not covered by the Assistance Board's

* The household income must be normally £400 a year or less (i.e., nearly £8 0s. 0d. per week or less).
† Your income in this case must be normally £250 a year or less (i.e., nearly £5 0s. 0d. per week or less) or £400 a year or less if you have dependants.
‡ You can get this form at your Town Hall or the offices of your Council.

3

---

scheme will be settled shortly, when Parliament has passed the War Damage Bill.

(3) If bombing has left you without any *ready cash*, because you have lost your job or cannot get to work to be paid or because you have been hurt, you can apply to the Assistance Board.

COMPENSATION FOR DAMAGE TO HOUSES

IF YOU *own your house* or hold it on a long lease and it is damaged or destroyed, whatever your income, you should, as soon as possible, make a claim on Form V.O.W.1.* The amount of your compensation and the time of paying it will depend on the passing of the War Damage Bill now before Parliament.

REPAIRS

IF YOUR HOUSE can be made fit to live in with a few simple repairs the local authority (apply to the Borough or Council Engineer) will put it right if the landlord is not able to do it. But how quickly the local authority can do this depends on local conditions.

FOOD

IF YOU should find it more convenient not to do your own cooking or you are unable to get gas, water or electricity, then in a rapidly increasing number of places you will find both before and after the raid community kitchens. Here you can get well cooked, hot meals at low prices in cheerful surroundings. If you prefer to do so you can buy the food ready cooked and take it home.

* You can get this form at your Town Hall or the offices of your Council.

4

You can find out if there are community kitchens in your town and where they are from any policeman, from the Town Hall or Council offices or the Citizens' Advice Bureaux.

THE INJURED

IF YOU are injured, treatment will be given at First Aid Posts and Hospitals, and :—
  (a) If your doctor says you are unable to work as a result of a "war injury," you will be eligible to receive an *injury allowance*. Application should be made immediately to the local office of the Assistance Board and you should take with you, or send, a medical certificate from a doctor or a hospital.
  (b) If you are afterwards found to be suffering from a serious and prolonged disablement, your case will be considered for a disability pension.
  (c) Widows of workers and Civil Defence Volunteers killed on duty will receive £2 10s. 0d. a week for ten weeks, after which a widow's pension will become payable. Pensions for orphans and dependent parents are also provided.
Ask at the Post Office for the address of the local branch of the Ministry of Pensions if you want to apply for a pension.

KEEP THIS AND DO WHAT IT TELLS YOU, HELP IS WAITING FOR YOU. THE GOVERNMENT, YOUR FELLOW CITIZENS AND YOUR NEIGHBOURS WILL SEE THAT "FRONT LINE" FIGHTERS ARE LOOKED AFTER !

Issued by the Ministry of Home Security in co-operation with the following Departments : The Treasury, the Ministry of Health, the Ministry of Pensions, the Ministry of Food and the Assistance Board.

51-8415 (2) H. B. & Co.

5

A leaflet we all hoped we would never need, anyway if the house was bombed we would be unlikely to find it.

To encourage patriotism, recruit personnel, to inform and to encourage thrift and reduce careless talk; Government advertising came in many forms. Leaflets, posters and as in this example on the lid of a milk bottle.

Paternal visits

I previously mentioned my father's cousin, Ruby and her husband Albert Horton, who ran a small grocery store on the Common. Last time I passed it, it was a café. She had two daughters some fifteen or so years older than myself but they had their own interests in life as young adult women are prone to do, and as my aunt was not enamoured of small boys, we did not spend much time with them.

As a result of this my mother must have been very lonely for much of the time, waiting for Thursday. With petrol unavailable to the general public it was fortunate for us that my father's visit was authorised on business grounds and equally lucky that he knew Kent so well. All road signs had been removed in May 1940 to handicap the enemy should they invade. On most Thursdays my father's delivery round to the Kent country bakers brought him about 2 o'clock to Lamberhurst, the farthest extremity of his territory. There were two bakeries in the village. These allowed him to see my mother and to meet my brother and me for a short while as we came out of school, sometimes for only a few minutes as he had a sixty mile journey to make to get back to Ramsgate in order be on duty in the fire station for the night. We looked forward to the event all day. In this respect we were extremely lucky although it did not seem so to us at the time. Many children were born after their fathers had been called up and had to wait until the war was over before even meeting them. That of course providing they had both survived.

This little letter was sent one week when my father was unable to visit us. As you see, the pictures are now war orientated with tanks, a barrage balloon lorry and army vehicles.

The paper is typical of the wartime supply with many discoloured particles in it.

Good manners and bad language

To break the monotony we caught the bus to Tunbridge Wells several times a year. As buses were few and far between they tended to be quite crowded. With no fuel for cars, public transport was in heavy demand, mostly for men either travelling to, or from work, or Forces personnel. In contrast to present day custom, men would immediately leap to their feet to offer my mother their seat. I offered mine to a young woman a few years ago. She looked at me as if I had gone completely mad and asked me if she looked like a bleeding cripple. I have seen that in Germany and Turkey this politeness survives. What happened here. Untravelled people in the Middle East still believe that the English are frightfully well mannered.

This brings another incident to mind. Bad language on television and films has led to it being assumed acceptable to everyone from small children, teenagers and young women who seem often to use it as much, or more, than their menfolk. Very many people would prefer a return to the days when it was totally unacceptable in mixed company. During one journey on the bus a man standing with his back to my mother referred to the "bloody" something or other. His neighbour nudged him and nodded in the direction of my mother. The man turned, saw Mother and went bright scarlet, apologising profusely. Swearing was never heard on the radio, or in films, in fact in both mediums the actors or interviewers spoke Oxford English unless they had character parts. Now there is nothing wrong with regional accents, but it does seem a shame that our children are hearing programmes

94

designed for them that the presenters often have little grasp of grammar and make errors like "Well he dunnit, init, t'morra." *(did it, isn't it, tomorrow).* We complain at the level of education of children. Poor little devils, how can schools compete in teaching correct usage of English to unwilling pupils who happily sponge up hours of devastatingly mis-pronounced language from their television superstars for the rest of their time. If they can't pronounce a word correctly how can they learn to spell it?

I remember my father telling me: "There are 33,000 words in the English language, surely you can find one that is better than a swear word?" Of course as children we heard and sometimes used "bloody" in a conversation with friends to show how worldly we were, but made sure there were no adults close by just as we did if we tried to smoke a cigarette, went scrumping for apples or playing ginger knock.

Ginger knock was the silly "game" of knocking on doors then running away. An advanced but more dangerous version was to tie a long length of string to the knockers of several houses in a row. Knock the first door, as it was opened it lifted the knocker on the next and as the door was angrily shut knocked the second and so on down the line. It seldom worked properly as we panicked at the thought of someone coming round the corner and catching us or a door opening as we tied the string. Few people had a door bell and if they did it was usually one where you pulled a knob connected to a wire which shook a bell inside the house.

Shopping trips

Our trips to Tunbridge Wells were often timed to come around Christmas or birthdays. There was only one toy shop in the town and we always visited it so that we could indicate what we hoped for, or where we spent money given by kind relations who had no idea what we would fancy. The choice was very, very limited and our expectations very undemanding compared with those of modern children. I still have a few books that were my Christmas or birthday present from my parents. By far the most lavish was a box of Reeves watercolour paints with a good brush when I was five or six. Many people buy cheap paints and brushes for their children. Cheap paints are discouraging, cheap brushes are total death to a child's aspirations. The bristles immediately bend at ninety degrees to the handle, like a mop. Turner himself could not have produced a painting with one, what chance has a child?

On our forays into the town I was told that, should I get lost, I was to go to the War Memorial in front of the Public Library and wait. On the left hand corner on the opposite side of the road was the Essoldo Cinema and it is still there. It was where I saw Bambi, newly issued by Walt Disney. This was my first experience of cinema. Before our move back to Ramsgate near the end of the war I was to also

95

see "Dumbo", "Lassie come Home" and "Lassie goes to War" the latter two being exceptional in that they were among the first films to be made live in Technicolor. Cartoons had been in colour for some time but most films were still in black and white. By the time I was nine I had seen four films. It was to be another seven years before I saw my first television, in black and white of course.

Other visits to that town were to climb on the rocks and to spend a day with a great-aunt who lived in Rusthall. She had another great nephew a few years older than me boarding with her as he attended Skinners School in Tunbridge Wells. He had constructed a beautiful model spitfire aircraft with wings of balsa wood covered with doped tissue. This had been painted so I had no idea it was fragile. She passed it to me for my inspection and I held it firmly by a wing punching holes straight through it. I was greatly embarrassed by the accident though on that occasion I did not meet him or have a chance to apologise. We finally did meet when we were both in our sixties. He politely disclaimed all memory of the incident.

Gardening

It is interesting to note that a 1936 30" (76cm) motor mower featured on the next page cost eighty pounds, between twenty and thirty weeks wages for a working man. Now a sit-on mower of that size would cost perhaps five or six weeks earnings.

The English have long been keen gardeners with flowerbeds and lawns encouraged by the efforts of Capability Brown and then Vita Sackville-West at Sissinghurst. Except for those with very large areas of grass, lawns in my youth were cut with a push along mower. One man or woman power. If the grass was more than a few inches long or slightly damp these machines clogged badly. I suspect it was the situation in this photo of my father (left). The mower would otherwise have a collecting bin on the front of it. With the need for food taking priority, lawns and road verges were often dug over to give way to vegetable production.

Food, especially that produced overseas, was in short supply and needed to be replaced by home grown product. Curiously there seems to have been enough sugar during those hard years. Previously from cane it now came from home grown sugar beet. Shipping faced great danger from enemy U-boat submarines. Germany was winning the battle. The loss of both ships and lives had been horrific so only essential goods were imported. Oranges and bananas were a thing of the past. Britain was obliged to grow its own food and, my goodness, as a result of an enormously successful "Dig for Victory" advertising campaign by the Government, they did just that. By 1943 privately grown fruit and vegetables totalled a million tons. Britons got slimmer, but healthier, with a low fat diet and plenty of fresh fruit and vegetables. We ate the produce of the season. When cabbages were gone we switched to lettuce. When strawberries finished they finished.

MOTOR LAWN MOWERS

are known to be efficient, strong, economical and extraordinary long-lived.

Expert investigation into turf culture results in the purchase of this machine, which is designed by engineers for the use of non-technical groundsmen and gardeners.
Improvements in details are to be observed in this year's pattern, notably the provision for an easy-starting refinement making rapid cranking quite unnecessary. An improved magneto shield is fitted. Lubrication of the clutch controls and of the front rollers is more readily effected, and the pram-type handle-bar gives easier control.
The specification retains the following valued features:—4½ h.p. 4-stroke engine with automatic pressure lubrication ; separate controls for driving and cutting ; ball-bearing gearbox ; enclosed drive; differential gears in driving roller.

24 in. - £70; 30 in. - £85;
36 in. - £100.

Trailer Seat for either model - - £6 10 0

The above prices are subject to 5% cash discount, and include free delivery to any Railway Station in Great Britain

A 16-page illustrated list will be supplied on request.

The choice for gardeners was between very expensive and very hard work. The Dennis machine was however built to last.

I have a friend who still uses one every week to keep his lawn immaculate so one could say his grandfather spent his money very wisely. The push-along mower has a roller but is heavy to work.

For country people with easy access to blackberries and apples, jam making was an opportunity too good to miss. Much of the fruit and vegetables picked was to be preserved. People did not live so much on tinned, or packaged food and there were in any case very few from which to choose. Each weekend in winter we were able to sit down to enjoy bottled blackberry and apple or rhubarb in a pie and overlook the toughness of the meat beneath homemade chutney. One way the weekly allowance of butter and margarine could be eked out was by using only jam on bread or toast. The saving of these fats allowed the making of pastry for fruit pies. Jam making was important. We furnished ourselves with hooks made by copying those used for hedging and ditching and scoured the area for berries. One source was in the gypsy camp sandpit described earlier, behind the Rising Sun on the opposite side of the Common, the pub is now renamed. I doubt if the efforts of my brother and I paid a dividend for my mother as we ate more than we put in our bowls and managed to spread juice all over our hands, faces and clothes.

Home preserved food for the winter provided welcome variety.

The Ministry of Food issued recipes for making low fat or zero fat cakes or cakes without egg in them. Eggs were in short supply, replaced by egg powder, flaked egg and no egg. Instead we had egg colouring powder, no egg in it at all, just a food dye, one a rather rich yellow and the other an almost luminous red. It kidded nobody but made things look a bit more attractive. I remember my mother making buns from a Ministry recipe, bits of potato had to be added to its no fat, no egg mix. I am unclear what the potato was to provide in the mix, however the buns got slightly overcooked and the bits of potato became nutty hard. Nut buns were at least a novelty but the experiment was never repeated.

Under the expert guidance of Mr Chandler my mother planted peas, runner beans, cabbages, sprouts, carrots and potatoes. I suppose my father dug over the garden but the weeding and watering was women's work. I was woken one fine summer evening to screams of laughter from the garden and looked out to see my mother and Mrs Chandler, finished with the gardening, having a battle using stirrup pumps in buckets.

The water fight

Stirrup pumps had been issued to houses to be used in the event of a fire caused by incendiary bombs. These were small bombs about a foot long, heavy enough to break through a roof tile and burst into fierce flame on impact. The pumps were designed with a support leg onto the floor, the bottom of it at ninety degrees for the operator's foot to hold it firmly on the ground and against a bucket while the pump part was within the bucket. They could either squirt out a fine spray or a jet of water. We never had cause to use them for their intended purpose. Air raids were not directed at small villages and we were anyway well outside ours; they were however very useful in the garden.

We had partridges come into the garden from the corn field beyond our hedge. They became a bit of a nuisance, scratching about and digging up vegetable seeds. Mrs Chandler told me the cure. All I had to do was creep up behind them and put a pinch of salt on their tail and I would easily catch them. I tried this a number of times, creeping quietly down between the runner beans so they wouldn't see me coming, then running the last bit to capture one. I have to say I now think I was mislead. Not all food was rationed. Rabbit and chicken were excluded though seldom available unless you kept your own. Here again country folk fared better than those in towns. Fish was also excluded as was whale meat, which became available at the end of the war.

Food and supplements

The Government had decreed that in order to ensure their health at a time when many foods were in short supply, or completely non-existent, children under two should receive a bottle of concentrated orange juice each week. This was later to include all pre-school age children while those of school age received a third of a pint of milk each school day. The orange juice had to be collected from the local Ministry of Food Office in return for coupons which were issued to parents of pre-school children. Me? I was difficult. I gave up milk at about three and absolutely refused to drink it. Bribery and threats alike had no effect and to this day I have a loathing of it, but love icecream.

School dinners, priced 2/1d (10p) per week, were another source of trouble. We were marched every lunchtime to a building on the opposite side of the road and occasionally I get whiff of over-boiled cabbage, or Brussels sprouts, that instantly brings the whole episode back to mind. I must have been a sad trial to my parents with my likes and dislikes. I enjoyed bacon and ate it whenever it was available. One day at the start of summer, and I remember it clearly, my mother said that she would not give me any that day as it was rather heavily salted. (This was done to help preserve it in a fridgeless society in the hotter weather.) When she next cooked it I refused to eat it and continued to refuse it for the next fifteen years. I've no idea why I took this stupid attitude. I also refused cheese and the fat on meat. At a time when all these were in short supply this must have meant that my parents had an excess of fat instead of lean meat and I an unfair share of the butter while they made do with my share of the cheese. Men on very heavy manual labour, like miners, got extra food to supplement their calory intake.

Each week we had a sweet ration allowance of between two and four ounces: ie: it varied over the years. The selection was somewhat limited by today's standard. There were aniseed balls, a maroon colour which changed to white after a few minutes sucking, boiled sweets like sherbet lemons, pear drops, fruit drops and Wilkinson's liquorish allsorts all loose in large glass jars, also liquorish comfits, liquorish bootlaces, liquorish pipes and dolly mixture. Sherbet came in paper tubes which one sucked up through a smaller liquorish tube. Rowntree's gums and pastilles were also available, my brother and I squabbled over the blackcurrant ones. That was it. It is interesting to note that all these are still available though now arriving in airtight packs untouched by the none to clean hand of the sweetshop lady as she groped around trying to separate the sticky items in their jar. Even so choosing was not easy. We were allowed two sweets each day after we had finished our dessert.

Flax

The property set in an orchard on the other side of Mrs Chandler's was owned by Mr Littlehaler, a smallholder who grew fruit trees and sold his produce in his small shop fronting on the lane. It was really a white-painted, weather-boarded shed. As often as not it was shut, but the fruit was left outside on display so that passers by could help themselves and leave the money in a tin. The pasture land behind him was suddenly ploughed up and hand sown with flax, a crop never grown in the area. During the war years the Ministry of Agriculture decided which farmers were to grow which crops, the amount being determined by national needs and the suitability of the land. That was the only time I have ever seen seed broadcast by hand in England. Before the introduction of seed drills all seed was distributed in that way.

The Sower

Flax has a very pretty pale blue flower and made a pleasant sight. We were told the stalks were destined to become linen of which the fat, 60'0" barrage balloons were being made. Linen and wool are the only natural fabric materials native to Britain. To be sure we made plenty of cotton material in the past, that was a benefit we derived from our Empire. Cotton producing countries sold their raw material to us, we had the machinery to convert it to cloth and resold it back to them as a finished product. In the first half of the 1940s cotton imports stopped so we were back to local basics.

Linen is a complicated product. The plant takes about a hundred days to grow. It must then be pulled from the ground either by machine, or by hand, to ensure the sap in the stalk does not dry out and weaken the inner fibres. The woody outer bark has then to be removed by boiling in alkali or oxalic acid and passed between rollers that disintegrate it; the waste is washed away. The inner fibres are combed out and spun into yarn and woven. In the past the bark was rotted away by soaking the plant for a week or two in a pond or stream then peeled off by hand.

Barrage Balloons

Barrage balloons were about 60ft long and 25ft in diameter and formed an 8,000ft fence around many towns and ports as they supported steel cables tethered to winches mounted on lorries or the ground. This obliged the enemy aircraft to fly high reducing the accuracy of their bombing. Over a hundred made the mistake of flying below the barrage and 66 came to grief as a result.

German Bombers

It is strange thinking back to what life was like. Of course we did not have Guy Fawkes night as the bonfires would have helped guide enemy aircraft to centres of population. However, sometimes I was woken by the sound of swarms of bombers going overhead at night on their way to attack the Medway towns or London. With the lights out my mother would open the blackout curtain and let me peep out of the window. We were quite high up and could see three ranges of hills stretching away to the north. Each had anti-aircraft guns, known as ack-ack guns, mounted on them. After the planes had passed us we could see their bluish exhausts and the many searchlights waving too and fro ahead of them trying to find them in the

German Dornier night time bombers flying over us on their way to London or the Medway towns. We could see them because their exhausts showed blue from the rear but the gunners, in front of them had to estimate their position and altitude then set their shells to explode at that guessed height.

blackness. Anti-aircraft guns fire very rapidly. To help the gunners know where their shells were going every few shells there was a tracer shell that shone like a rocket, they made a dotted line in the sky as they seemed to arc slowly up towards the planes. It was all very impressive to look at from a safe distance. Radar was then insufficiently developed for it to guide the gunnery crew. Watching was a special treat, but I had nightmares for many years after the war. Dreaming of the blue exhaust lights and seeing these planes circling round to come back to bomb me. The effects of war do not stop when the fighting finishes.

One day a fighter shot down a plane close to us, the pilot escaping by parachute. We watched him floating down until he disappeared behind the trees several hundred yards away. Five minutes later an army jeep came roaring past to capture him, but he had already been caught by a farm worker with a pitchfork. The German was probably very relieved to see the army in the circumstances. Bundled into the jeep he passed us with the soldiers cheering and waving to us as they returned to the village.

102

D-Day preparations

Roughly half way between Ramsgate and Sandwich lies the hamlet of Ebbsfleet and the WW1 secret port of Richborough. There were still two large dock cranes and a slipway served by a substantial railway network on both sides of the road and during the latter days of WW2 it became the storage and launching point for parts of the Mulberry Harbour, the instant floating dock to be used for the D-Day landings. They were to be towed across the Channel to form the harbour for ships carrying the troops and equipment when the invasion started.

When we visited my grandparents for a break the top deck of the buses between Ramsgate and Sandwich were whitewashed over so that one could see almost nothing out of their windows. Kids being kids we did try and it was possible to make out huge, weird shapes on the railway trucks. The sidings stretched away towards Richborough castle, the old Roman fortress built to guard the Channel that in former times flowed between the island of Thanet and the mainland. The railway crossed the road opposite Richborough's post-war power station *(now the distribution point for electricity generated by the marine wind farm several miles east of Margate)* and fed into a substantial shunting yard and dock on the seaward side of the road.

A common sight during the war years was a bomber towing up to three large gliders each carrying 16 men or equipment. Normally these gliders were towed off the ground at an airfield, but it was possible to make a snatch take-off and I once saw this done. Two long poles were put in the ground well apart and a looped towline from the glider was taken forward and supported between the poles. A large bomber then flew over low down with a trailing hook which caught the stretched line and jerked the glider and its crew into instant flight. 0-110 mph in seven seconds. Very impressive to watch, I understand it was common practice because gliders have very little choice about where they land and any space will do when you are running out of altitude and under enemy fire. Having discharged their load the next thing was to get back home for the next load. During some actions, like the battle at Arnhem, (subject of the film "A Bridge Too Far") there was insufficient space and many, without any choice, ran into those already landed, or rammed natural obstacles. It was my grandfather's great nephew, Robert Cain, who held the bridge and was the only soldier in that battle awarded Britain's highest military honour, the Victoria Cross, and to survive.

We had become used to seeing army troop manoeuvres, convoys of lorries, brengun carriers, mobile guns, tanks and tank transporters trundling around the countryside. A week or so before D-Day, the invasion of France, there was a large increase in the number of soldiers marching into the village, convoys of equip-ment and their crews suddenly arrived and parked in the surrounding orchards. Mobile kitchens sprang up in Mr Littlehaler's orchard to feed the influx of men and it was clear to us that something important was about to happen. Then suddenly one morning we woke to find the place was empty. Gone were the men and the vehicles, like magic. Overnight the place had become once again a sleepy village. Now a seemingly endless flood of bombers and gliders crowded the sky above us on their way to assist the invasion. It was so good to see bombers going in the opposite direction. Just inside our garden gate in a brown paper bag was a collection of brass army cap and shoulder badges, the currency of small boys. One of the soldiers had obviously noticed us and, lacking the chance to give them to his own children had left them for us. I have frequently thought of this kind, unknown man. What happened to him? Did he survive the war? Alive or dead, it is of him I think every November on Remembrance Day.

Doodlebugs

Thursday 22 June 1944. On the way to school with my brother we were climbing over the style before the hop garden when we heard a strange aircraft making a sort of rapid burping noise. On the basis that I knew what our planes sounded like, I decided this was probably German so we ran the rest of the way. On arrival we found everyone in the air raid shelter and a few minutes later there was a loud explosion. It was the beginning of the V1 rocket attacks. Pilotless 2,000kg rocket bombs which we came to call "doodlebugs". The Germans had yet to work out exactly how much fuel they needed to reach London, their intended target, but by the end of the month they were sending about 50 a day. We soon got used to seeing them pass overhead. There was no danger until their motor stopped, then they

A doodlebug in the sights of a spitfire

dived, sometimes giving a little upwards nod before diving. If nearby one then had about 15 seconds in which to take cover. Our instructions were to get down in a ditch if we thought they would land anywhere close to us as the blast would then pass over us. I had the chance to try out this advice. I had reached Mr Littlehaler's shop when I saw a doodlebug on a much lower flight path than usual, apparently heading for our chimney. Terrified for my mother indoors I flung myself into the ditch, very grateful that it was dry and had been newly cleaned by the roadman. Luckily it passed without incident. My mother and I stood together on our front door step watching its flight to Tunbridge Wells, where it ran smack into a barrage balloon and exploded in a spectacular ball of flame in the released hydrogen.

The website http://www.1940.co.uk/history/sound/sound.htm has sounds from the era which include an air raid. It should be listened to in the dark, as loud as possible while trying to imagine that you are the target. That is how they were heard by us. There is also the sound of a doodlebug. In this instance the time lag between the engine stopping and the explosion is 12 seconds.

Shortly after this we had another incident. In an attempt to save comparatively densely populated London, fighter aircraft were instructed to shoot down doodle-bugs over the relatively unpopulated area between the coast and the metropolis. A Spitfire dived on one flying towards us. I ran inside the house, but my brother, Michael, stood for a minute to watch until our other neighbour, Mrs Smith, shouted to him to get indoors. The moment he stepped back through the doorway a red hot section of the Spitfire's cannon shell landed on the spot he had just vacated.

About this time, and I suppose as a result of the near disaster, my parents bought a Morrison shelter. You are right, they were not a pretty sight. They took the form of a steel table topped with an eighth inck thick steel sheet and sides protected by a grill similar to that used now in reinforced concrete floors. There was room under it for two adults and they earned a great reputation for saving lives as they could withstand the weight of a house collapsing on top of them. My brother and I then slept under it in the dining room, but my mother continued to use her bed only coming down if she heard gunfire. The final straw came when Mrs Chandler had a shell through her half of the roof in a similar doodlebug action. Mid-Kent had become more dangerous than Ramsgate from "friendly" gunfire now that the Germans were in retreat. We said goodbye to Lamberhurst, I with great regret as I was now a country boy with country interests and no wish to become a "Towney" as the country people called town dwellers.

Reconstruction of a Morrison table with its front grill removed, practical but not very beautiful.

This is the fire engine, made by Johillco, competing with Dinky immediately before the war. The company seems to have disappeared. It was very nicely made with detachable firemen, very similar to Ramsgate's fire engine of that period with the men sitting on the side and the brass bell.

There seems often to have been distrust between country folk and town dwellers, each thinking the other inferior. Town people seeing their country cousins as unsophisticated, leading boring lives, herding animals from field to field. Meanwhile the countrymen regard townsfolk as city slickers unable to appreciate the quiet, slower pace of life, ignorant of the names of plants and birds, content to trudge to the same office or workshop in the hurly burly of traffic and crowds and getting their daily dose of pollution. Farmers are, of necessity, some of the most multi-skilled and resourceful people one can meet, needing an understanding of plant biology, soil chemistry, electricity, building, plumbing, engineering and welding skills and considerable veterinary ability. I had a temporary secretary at one point in my career who asked me why on earth I lived in the country with nothing to look at but trees and grass. I asked her what she found so appealing about watching the rain dripping from the newsagent's sunblind opposite her house when in the sticks I could see the daily scene change as the seasons progressed. But there you go ... some like the crowds, cafes and instant access to shops. Others prefer to hear an owl hooting and see the stars without light pollution, but perhaps needing to think a day or two in advance for shopping needs.

Back to Picton Road

For a short while we stayed once more in Sandwich to give my parents time to get their house cleaned up and the furniture out of storage. When we arrived back to Picton Road I ran into the house straight to my toy cupboard, and sure enough my little fire engine with its six firemen was waiting for me under a light covering of dust. The kitchen was much more convenient for my mother. Back with her gas cooker and hot water from the coke fired stove, but by present day standards a 1945 kitchen was pretty basic. In company with the bulk of the population we had no central heating. Open coal, or gas fires, were the norm in the livingroom and front room, lit only when necessary because of the fuel shortages and costs.

Beyond the kitchen was usually a scullery where the washing was done. Also a larder, a small, ventilated room or cupboard where food was stored. Where practicable this was on the north side of the house to keep things as cool as possible. This was the case in our house. The back addition beyond the scullery divided into three. To the right, the larder, to the left the side and rear wall of the outside toilet with the passage to the back door in between them. Building regulations thirty years later still insisted on a ventilated cupboard for food storage as a condition for obtaining a Government Improvement Grant, but the vent was quite unnecessary as by then almost everyone had a fridge and most, a deep freeze as well. People just blocked up the draughty vent as soon as the Building Inspector had gone away.

Our kitchen was long enough to double as the dining room, the table and chairs being in the position of the pastry table in my illustration overleaf. It held the gas cooker, (some people now had electric), a white porcelain sink with a wooden draining board hooked on the end. Also a gas fired Burco boiler in which the laundry was boiled in Persil prior to being rinsed in the sink or a tin bath in the garden. In wet weather clothes could hang from the ceiling rack and as with every room in most homes, the whole was lit by one 100w bulb in the centre of the room.

The floor was cement, covered with an eighth of an inch thick sheet of brown cork composition called linoleum. None of it was very beautiful, but it was practical, clean, comparatively cheap to run and people's expectations were much more modest than nowadays. The cleaning equipment was kept hooked to the wall just behind the door down to the coal cellar, it comprised a vacuum cleaner, brush and a carpet sweeper. Seldom seen nowadays, these were very practical for a quick push round and less cumbersome than a Hoover. The following year, 1946, my second brother was born and my mother bought a small appliance to mince food for him, I believe that was our first electric kitchen appliance.

Carpet - -
Sweepers

No Home
Complete
Without
One

THE BENEFIT OF A CARPET SWEEPER

Arises from the ease and speed with which it does the work. It causes neither stooping nor backache, and does not permit any dust to escape into the room. The sweeping is done more thoroughly than that done by a broom under the most favourable conditions ; and it is less troublesome, inasmuch as the sweepings are taken right out of the carpet into the machine, and so carried completely away.

The style of this advertisement suggests it was from Victorian times but ours was bought in 1934, the year of my parents' marriage.

Our toast was made under the cooker grill. Heating and all hot water came from the coke stove and was another reaon to eat in the kitchen. Its annual decoration was cream distemper, a mixture of lime, water and a stainer to produce the desired colour. Very cheap and easy to use but inclined to crack and peel off; it was to provide the next two generations of decorators with the wearying task of dissolving it off as the surface. The new plastic paints broke the tenuous grip of the distemper from the wall plaster as they dried. Redecoration often took care of one week of a man's two weeks annual holiday.

At first I know I resented having my father about all the time. My mother would smack us if we were very naughty, but I quickly found that, although quite fair, my father's hand was larger and heavier when he took over control again. I think maybe this resentment led me to be a bit of a pain over the next few years.

A coke hod and a boiler for heating the room, cooking and hot water.

The house needed total redecoration after being empty and unheated for so many years. Some window sash cords required replacement. Mr Swaffer, an elderly, local carpenter who did various jobs for my grandfather came to effect the repairs. He was a real character and the uncle of Hannan Swaffer, a well known journalist of the period

A kitchen of the 1940s.

who was awarded Granada Foreign Correspondent of the Decade in 1965 and Journalist of the Year in 1966. Mr Swaffer's association with my grandpa probably went back fifty years and they almost always argued furiously about how things should be done. Mr Swaffer claimed to be a rough carpenter, but was in fact a skilled cabinetmaker on the quiet. He built veneered cocktail cabinets for his relations and made beautiful violins to amuse himself, but was sadly lacking any aesthetic sense. His joinery was impeccable, but he stained the violins with dark wood stain and failed to varnish them. He was a bit gruffly spoken; as a nine year-old I was a little frightened of him but fascinated watching him work. His home in St Lawrence was squeezed between the Wheatsheaf and Mr Siminson's pharmacy. His workshop in its high-walled garden was attached to the back of his house like a lean-to. It had small-paned greenhouse type windows to give maximum light all along the outside, typical of a carpenter's shop of those times. It looked out at a magnificent, centuries old mulberry tree with its lengthy branches supported on poles. Sadly the tree, which supplied mulberry leaves for my silkworms, has now followed its owner. Dismantling our sitting-room box sash window he gruffly said to me: "Make sure you remember how to do this. I don't expect to have to do it again". It must have made a considerable impression on me because, although I had no need to do this job until I was in my middle thirties, I remembered the whole operation like a newly watched film.

Speaking of Mr Siminson reminds me that during sweet rationing I used to visit his pharmacy to buy Parma violet breath sweeteners which were not rationed and a bit like Dolly mixture. One day I made the stupid mistake of buying Ex-Lax chocolate. I understood chocolate, but failed to comprehend the Ex-Lax part. I learnt by experience.

Mr Siminson was not only a chemist, but also a newsagent and stationer, and an excellent amateur photographer who provided the local papers with many of their pictures. On one side of his shop was an untidy mess of papers, periodicals, comics and photographs stacked higgledy piggledy on the counter. To ask for a back number of "Radio Fun", "Hotspur", or "Beano" was to start a formidable search operation. This was really Mrs Siminson's department and she had to be summoned from her kitchen at the back of the shop, behind the dispensary, to assist. Her assistance had limitations however, for though she was geniality personified, she was enormous and half filled the shop. It was probable that the object of the search was not on the counter at all but in the middle of another stack of papers which occupied the shop chair, but she was unable to stoop down low enough to see.

There were nearly always several people awaiting their turn to be served on the chemist's counter which ran down the other side of the room. Before 1948 there was no National Health Service. Visits to the doctor were expensive and Mr Siminson was almost as good. Or at any rate the results which he achieved were every bit as good, because he was a great psychologist. He listened while the sufferer described his pain, and when it started, and how it affected him, and would then ask one or two questions before proclaiming: "I've got the very thing for you! Just what you want! It will get right into you and cure you in no time! You'll feel better after the first dose and by the morning the pain will have disappeared." And it often did.

Interior decoration

Interior decoration of the time was largely simple wallpaper with panels of border, the upper corners of which had a decorative motif stuck on to join up the plain vertical and top horizontal border strips. *(See the icon above and the illustration on page 137)*. Fitted carpets had not been born. A standard size rectangular carpet was laid leaving a foot or eighteen inch space all round; this area was either stained dark brown or covered with linoleum. Decoration was mostly done by tradesmen who really knew their job. Until the fifties, with the relaxation of restrictions, new modern materials and tools for do-it-yourselfers were unavailable. Ceilings, kitchens and utility rooms were painted with a mixture of lime and colour stains and woodwork with oil based paint each coat of which took a day, or two, to dry. Acrylic paint had not yet been invented. Outside woodwork of buildings was treated with long lasting, lead based paints that are now forbidden in case children go mad and happen to chew the window sill or skirting board. Front doors were frequently stained and grained to resemble wood of much higher quality than that actually used in their construction and the lower part of the entrance walls often painted to resemble marble. Halls and staircases had sturdy Lincrusta embossed wallpaper up to the 1.20m mark. Arts that almost died but have in recent years achieved a comeback in interior design. Now done by specialist, arty painters who expect all the preparatory work to be done before they arrive and charge out of all relationship to the work involved. I have done plenty so I do know what I'm talking about.

Dentists

During the years in Lamberhurst my second teeth had arrived in a jumble and were crowding my narrow jaws. As a precaution against later problems I was blessed with extra canines top and bottom to add to the confusion. I suppose the local dentist had been called up with the outbreak of war and been replaced by a woman who had maybe been thrown into the job before gaining enough experience. To reduce the crowding in my mouth she managed to pull out a second tooth, leaving a milk tooth. As a result I later became a showpiece each time I went to a new dentist. The milk tooth finally fell out when I was fifty-one.

On our return to Ramsgate my father took me to an old dentist living opposite using his front room as a surgery; a heavy smoker, oblivious to the state of his breath as he peered into my mouth. He was a veritable butcher, without sympathy. His tooth drilling machine was operated by foot like an old Singer sewing machine. He swayed slightly as he pedalled the drill so that his pressure wavered between light and enough to push the offending tooth out of its socket. Added to his economy with anaesthetic and foul breath, a visit to him could best be described as unforgettable.

This same ungentle gentleman fitted me with upper and lower plates, like those that stared out of a glass beside my grandparents' bed, but instead of teeth it had adjustable pegs which pressed firmly against my crooked teeth. These eventually twisted straighter but I hated the things and eventually dropped them down a friendly street drain. As a result my teeth are still slightly crooked but I expect in due course I shall, with the wonders of modern technology, have a smart, straight new set on pegs screwed into my jaw bones and nobody will recognise me.

A dentists's foot operated drill.

POST-WAR

Please turn to next page....

Finally the war finished

Finally on 7 May 1945 the war in Europe ended although the struggle against the Japanese continued until 15 August 1945. Hitler had committed suicide to the delight of all except those who would have preferred to take him to pieces little bit by little bit. That evening my father took me to walk along the West Cliff and down to the harbour to see all the street lighting now switched back on for the first time since the outbreak of war. For me it was like magic, now nine-years-old, I had no memory of having seen so much lighting before being only three the last time it was used.

Otherwise not much changed. Britain had been short of food and restricted as to diet, but Europe was in a much worse state. The Dutch were starving as were the millions of refugees in other European countries. Priority had to be given to them before restrictions could be relaxed and supplies reorganised.

There were a number of elderly people in the town who had lived permanently down the air raid tunnels throughout the war only venturing out to do their shopping. Two old ladies living a few doors from us were like that. When the war was over they came home again but were a strange yellowy grey colour, like ghosts, from the lack of daylight.

The Ramsgate tunnels which led down to the beach below the East Cliff were subsequently modified to carry a new sewage system.

British Prisoners of War

There had been partial exchanges of prisoners during the hostilities, usually men injured and unlikely to rejoin the combat. Now servicemen and those who had been prisoners of the Germans, or Japanese, some for many years, were brought home. To celebrate their return street parties were held outside their houses. All the neighbours brought their tables out into the middle of the road to form a long line, flags and bunting were strung across both ends of the street; Union Jacks and great banners saying Welcome home Bill or Jack in two foot high letters. The outside of the houses were also similarly decorated. There were several in roads around us. Many of the men were in poor health, those from the Far East in particular. Thirty years later I became friendly with an ex Lt Colonel in the Intelligence Corps who had been a prisoner of the Japanese in the notorious Changhi prison camp. He looked fifteen years older than his age and still suffered regular recurrences of malaria and dysentery. The film "The Bridge over the River Kwai" illustrates the sort of treatment these men had received.

Men who had served out there, but escaped capture, were easily recognisable as the quinine tablets they had been obliged to take to ward off malaria had caused them to have the appearance of jaundice. Both their skin and the whites of their eyes had become yellow; it wore off over a period of months.

113

St Laurence Boys' School

Of course I had to go to school. My parents chose St Laurence School for Boys opposite the school for girls in Newington Road. Both buildings have disappeared now, but were church schools with very good academic records. We congregated in the playground each morning until "Tiddly" Watson, the headmaster, came onto the top step and blew his whistle. The signal to stop moving. Nicknamed "Tiddly", because of his tiddly stick for use on the behinds, or hands, of those foolish enough to excite his displeasure. A second blast and we had to form up in separate lines for each class and solemnly walk up the steps into the single storey building. For a time I was taught by Miss Lacey in Standard 1 but I think that

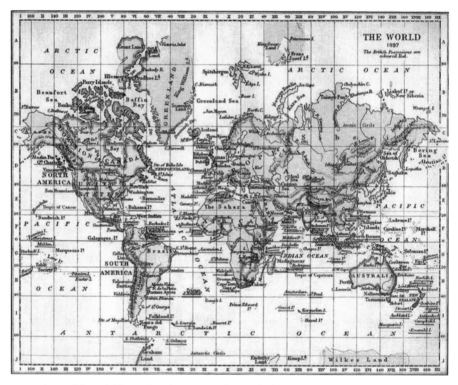

Map of the British Empire shown in pink, on which we learned the sun never set.

was during a period when the Standard 2 teacher, Mr Williamson was away for some reason. The only thing I remember learning from her was the Creed: "I believe in God the Father Almighty etc". Not a requirement in the Methodist Chapel of my parents. She ferocious unlike Mr Williamson who was a very kindly man, he encouraged me and lent me books if I appeared interested in them. In his class I was introduced to long division of pounds, shillings and pence, and the mysteries of yards, rods, chains and furlongs. We also learnt the old folk song: "Early one morning, just as the sun was rising, I heard a maiden singing in the valley below. Oh, don't deceive me. Oh, never leave me. How could you treat a poor maiden so". I think the song would have been better learnt a few years later

114

when we might have understood its import. It was in this class that I met Brian Sparkes who was to become a lifelong friend although our paths led in very different directions.

The following year, Standard 3, ten-year-olds, and our teacher was Mr Stanley. We sat in order of our academic success. In our class of about thirty members I ranked fifth so sat in the third desk back. Desks were of oak, in pairs, in lines of seven, or eight, deep with a passageway between each line. The teacher wrote in white chalk on the black-board. So called because they were just that, black, and stood on an easel. It had a roll of song sheets printed large enough to be seen from the back of the class mounted above it and they were flopped over the front when we were to learn one. His only other teaching aid was a large wall map of the British Empire. The oak desks had a flat strip across the top then the flap sloped slightly towards the pupil. The flat top had a half round groove in it to house pens and pencils and an inkwell set into the right hand side. Fountain pens were expensive. No we did not use quills, we had penholders with steel nibs which we dipped in the ink just like Charles Dickens. Ballpoint pens or corrector fluid had yet to be invented. Blots and smears were easily made, but impossible to erase and cost marks for untidy work. It was during my last year at this school that I heard for the for the first time of a new type of pen being used by airmen which did not freeze at high altitudes and lasted for a year. This magic pen came on sale to the public later in the year, 1946. The Biro. They have been produced by the billion. I can't understand why we are not tramping through redundant ballpoints in the street. Where do they all go? Most desks had been carved or scratched under the lid with the initials of previous occupants and appeared to be generations old. Occasionally a particularly good piece of work would be pinned up on the wall as a sort of reward for good work. I remember having a drawing of a squirrel hung there.

A typical oak double desk of the era and a good many years before it.

Nationalism

The fact that we had won the war, together with the map on the walls of most schools in the country showing a quarter of the world coloured red, combined to give us a feeling of great national pride. These red areas were the countries that formed the British Commonwealth, our empire, the largest empire the world had ever seen. All Canada, India and what is now Pakistan, huge chunks of Africa, all Australia, New Zealand, a bit of South America, Malaya, Hong Kong, Singapore, and just about every strategically important island in the world. We were members of the most influential empire in the history of our universe, had stood against the German nation when France and Belgium had given up, surrendered. Certainly the Americans had helped, eventually; but we had held the enemy at bay at enormous cost with the help of our Empire. National pride at having done this twice in thirty years was enormous. National pride is sadly something that we seem to have lost over the past seventy years. I think it a great shame because it is reflected in many ways. A general lowering of standards, a carelessness in personal and business relationships and the loss of good manners. Things for which the British were famous. Pride in being independent and not living on charity for instance. When Old Age pensions were introduced many elderly people refused them because they saw the money as a kind of charity. To accept it indicated you could not manage alone and that was a form of disgrace. Now children leaving school are fully equipped with the knowledge of how to get as much as possible from the State for the least amount of effort. Pride in independence has largely gone.

Of course there was a price to pay for the assistance given to us by the Commonwealth countries. They had fought as hard as us, suffered as we had in many cases and now expected our respect, not a return to subservience to the Great White King over the water. They were as good as us when it came to a fight and they wanted independence. And eventually they either got it or took it.

Vandalism and high spirits

The shortest way to school was to cross Ellington Park. It was ruled by the Park Keeper who carried a pointed stick designed to collect any paper blowing about the place. He saw it as his duty to try to stop us climbing the oak, walnut, horse chestnut and elm trees that bordered parts of his domain. This was long before Dutch elm disease which wiped out almost all the elms in Britain. These trees had been planted generations before when the park was a private estate. The estate had formerly been the home of a man who had gone mad and killed his wife and six dogs in Georgian times. We would make sure that "Parky" was out of sight and then try to climb to the top of the tree, where the rooks had made their homes. One could never get to the nests as at that level the branches were too thin to support us. We just wanted to carve our initials as high as possible to prove we had been there. I saw one boy climbing down from a similar foray while

the park keeper stabbed at his descending rear with the pointed stick which I thought was taking very unfair advantage.

Thinking of this unfairness the next day I amused myself by plodding down a newly planted row of pansies watching carefully to see that I had obliterated each one. Looking up at the end of the row I found myself face to face with "Specs", the under park keeper. You may not have much trouble guessing why he was known by this name to all the children. He of course recognised me and marched me home to tell my father of my sin. I forget the outcome, but suspect Father paid the cost of the plants and stopped my sixpence a week pocket money to reimburse himself.

As darkness fell a bell at the side of "Parky's" house was rung as a signal to leave the grounds before the gates were shut. This was late during the summer but about 4.20 pm in mid-winter. A pointless operation for some years after the war as the railings that had surrounded half the parkland had been

116

taken for scrap iron at the start of hostilities. For fun, and to annoy "Parky" we hid in the shrubbery on the walled side until he had passed by and locked the last gate which adjoined his house. We then crept up his short garden path and rang the bell and ran for it, climbing over the old flint wall and walking nonchalantly along the road. Silly, childish stuff but it amused us to think of it annoying him.

There were plenty of buildings destroyed or semi-destroyed in the town. These bomb-sites as they were known were magnets for small boys. The danger came not from those buildings that had been flattened like those in Wilfred Road opposite my grandfather's house. Hit on 12 February 1941 by a landmine parachuted down, its blast had not been muffled by being down a hole. The sideways blast had destroyed six houses instead of the normal one or two and blew in the front door of my Grandpa's house. No, we were interested in those dilapidated buildings with the stairs hanging half off the wall or large sections of floor missing leaving interesting holes into which we could climb.

Our heroes were commandos. If the war had lasted we would have been commandos. These were to be our training ground, scrambling from room to room across floors now pitched at crazy angles, looking for whatever had survived the devastation of someone's

The flint wall behind "Specs" is a very fine example of knapped flintwork; flint occurs in layers of chalk and is about as hard as glass. Knapping is chipping stone to shape. These stones are squared on five faces. It is not easy to knap flint on two faces, five faces is very skilled work. The stone ballustrade has now gone, replaced by cheap iron railings.

home or business. These buildings had been boarded up but in due time the boards had become loose, probably with a little help from others like us. Looking back I can see that we were extraordinarily lucky not to have killed ourselves. There was a Baptist Church in Chapel Place with its gallery half off the wall and large sections missing, the object of a direct hit. I used to climb around it and try with my Webley air pistol to shoot the ducks waddling about far below in the back garden of a house behind it. In fact the only danger for the ducks at that distance was accidentally eating a pellet and suffering from lead poisoning. There was a curious, nice thing about bomb sites; they seemed always to grow buddleias and elder trees in no time at all and were a haven for Red Admiral butterflies.

Refugees

Many hundreds of thousands of displaced people throughout the continent finished the war in places far from their homes. Members of families were completely separated from each other not knowing where husbands, wives or children were or even if they were alive. In many cases they were not, having been herded into German or Russian labour camps or to the gas chambers, or killed in the fighting, or bombing.

While living in Israel I met a Czechoslovakian woman who had been taken prisoner by Russian forces and sent to a Labour Camp. This in turn had been over-run by the Germans who sent her to Poland to a similar camp. When the war ended the Americans rounded her up with other released labourers and interned her to another country in a refugee camp. She was working at my local supermarket and asked which language I preferred to speak. This surprised me as I have not met many multilingual supermarket cashiers so I asked how many she spoke. She replied "Only seven properly" and then I learnt her story. She had never found the rest of her family. Grandparents, parents, brothers and sisters, cousins, uncles, gone…all gone. Sadly I met many others there in the same tragic state. Even in Britain soldiers returned to find their house, and often the surrounding streets, had been entirely wiped out. The surviving residents dispersed to temporary accommodation, relocated to another part of the country to work, their wife's relocation letter to her husband destroyed when the ship carrying it was sunk.

I watched a recent TV programme in which two sisters separated at the beginning of the war were reunited for the first time in seventy years. The task of tracing relatives was enormous. Colonel Menzies, later my swimming instructor, *(mentioned on p30)* spent a number of post-war years in Europe with aid agencies helping to restore survivors to their loved ones.

The state of the country

Transport of goods from America and Asia required ships. It took time to replace the huge loss of vessels during the war years. Our shipyards were worn out producing battleships and submarines and had been severely bombed. Reconstruction took time, during which the Germans and the Japanese received vast financial aid for reconstruction from America under what was called the Marshall Plan. Their industrial and ship building capacity totally destroyed during the conflict was now being rebuilt. New! The latest technology! In England we had not suffered this complete annihilation so instead of rebuilding there was a cobbling together, a patching up of what remained. This together with many strikes and aggressive, avaricious trade unions left England and themselves the losers. Our manufacturing and shipbuilding supremacy has been taken by other countries and we have largely become a nation of stockists and distributors in those vital areas. In retrospect it would seem that the Germans and Japanese won the war or at least benefitted most from its outcome. Sixty years on we are placed as the world's seventh industrial nation with overseas companies actually owning much of it.

With peace restored, did we rush to the beach to swim? No chance at all. Miles of beach and foreshore were heavily seeded with mines laid in haste with far from careful plans and in any case the scaffolding and barbed wire defences were still in place. The sea had many mines anchored as a protection around port entrances or positions designed to cause maximum damage to an invading force. In bad storms it was not uncommon for one to break free and bob its way gently onto the beach, to explode if it hit awkwardly, blowing out the windows of nearby buildings, or to float free down the Channel to the considerable hazard of shipping. It was to take long and careful clearance to make the seashore safe for

A short length of Sandwich Bay beach re-opened and free of mines.

holidaymakers. The first 100 yards or so of local beach to be cleared was in Sandwich Bay. What delighted kids we were to once more get our feet wet and build sand castles on that first available Saturday. When Ramsgate's main sands had been cleared I chanced upon a container of strange, thin ropey material. I called a policeman who came with a bucket of water into which the container was duly sunk and carted away. He came to the house later to thank me and said it was gun cotton, a highly explosive mix of cordite and nitroglycerin apparently fallen from a ship.

Housing

Demobbed troops returning to wives they had not seen for a long time celebrated by producing the children they had planned to have before being called up. What has since been labelled the Baby Boom resulted in a greatly increased population. This, combined with over 2,250,000 houses destroyed or damaged, caused an acute shortage of homes. Adult married children were crowded into the small houses and flats of their parents. Building materials were in very short supply so that make-do and mend was the order of the day rather than proper repairs. About four million homes were without bathrooms, hot water or electricity and few had central heating. Twenty years later I visited a Folkestone house still lit by gas. Coal or gas fires provided heat. The kitchen coal or coke fired back boiler or an Ascot gas fired water heater were the usual means of heating water for those who had a bathroom.

Prefabs were not a very pretty sight unless you were homeless or obliged to live in very crowded accommodation with your in-laws. For such people they were heaven and they came with the luxury of a built in, gas operated refrigerator.

To alleviate the crisis the Government ordered the construction of prefabs. These small, single storey houses, 9m x 7m, needed only a concrete base with the normal services connected. The rest arrived in sections; the walls and flat roofs that were bolted together on site. Built in days rather than months they were intended to last twelve to fifteen years and by the time construction stopped in 1949 more than 156,500 stood around the country. Sixty years later people are fighting to retain as treasured homes those not already destroyed. I remember walking, together with many others, to the Newington Estate one Sunday afternoon to view the first three to be erected in Ramsgate. The previous week there had been just a row of concrete slabs, now there were three homes. It was incredible. Shortly after this the Government brought out two storey houses that could be rapidly built as pairs or terraces. These were better quality than the prefabs having a pebble-dashed, precast concrete weatherboard exterior. Intended to be replaced after twenty-five years, there are plenty of them still in use today. With roses growing across the walls, they now blend in quite nicely with the usual mixed village architecture though I know nothing of their interior wear and tear.

120

This Huguenot house was built by Dutch refugees in the 1700s to house one family. These two pictures taken almost fifty years apart illustrate how large houses have been modified to form smaller units without destroying the original character of the exterior of the building which remains unchanged except for one window converted into a doorway and the bay window and porch added in Victorian times. The house is actually L shaped, the remainder hidden round the corner behind the bay tree and now provides four homes.

Surveys after the war showed that most people hoped to have a house with a garden. The Labour Government totally ignored their wishes and under the influence of the architect Corbusier started erecting high rise buildings. A serious error which is only now being expensively redressed by spectacular explosive demolition. They were for the most part an unmitigated disaster as homes for young families, because of lift failures, vandalism and lack of private play space for either small children or teenagers, the latter left to wander the streets. To make way for these monstrosities great numbers of Victorian terrace houses, missed by the bombing, were demolished instead of being renovated at considerably lower cost. Those not destroyed are now very valuable housing stock.

As more and more "Do-it-yourself" tools and materials became available, people started to buy delapidated properties and renovate them, sell, then move upmarket and repeat the operation. Larger houses were split into bedsits, studios and flats. Those with large gardens were bulldozed away and small estates took their place. The British were changing from renters to house owners. By 1961 house owners outnumbered those in private rented property for the first time. When Prime Minister Margaret Thatcher allowed the selling of council houses home ownership shot to over 70%. My early venture into this market about forty years ago cost me £4,500, That property is now around £250,000. Maybe now there will be a return to rental as prices escalate beyond the reach of young people.

121

Lavatories, toilets, loos

Whatever you call them, after the war, in hundreds of thousands of British homes they lay outside the back door. Even in 1978 my next door neighbours, in London's Wandsworth, still insisted that inside toilets were unhealthy and, rain or shine, stuck to their outside loo. For night time use there was a potty referred to as a "gzunder" because it "goes under" the bed, or a "Jerry" because its shape resembled a German army helmet. Public toilet cubicles' doors had a large brass lock on the outside with a slot in the top. To gain entry one put a penny in the slot. This gave rise to the common euphemism "Just a minute, I want to go and spend a penny".

Thomas Crapper

Born in 1836, he was apprenticed to a plumber. At 25 he set up his own business. Such was his skill and inventiveness that he developed a trap that stopped the smell of the drains returning. His fame spread and in the 1880s he was asked to supply the Prince of Wales with toilets for Sandringham, Windsor Castle, Buckingham Palace and Westminster Abbey. He died in 1920 but his name and products go on.

Fuels

Kent had four coalmines and a large number of Welsh miners who had moved in with their expertise to work them. Major users of the coal were the local gas works and Ramsgate's had taken quite a pasting from an air raid designed to shut it down. Unfortunately the inhabitants of the nearby streets bore the brunt of the attack and many people had been killed. My father was one of those who helped fight the fire. The gasworks survived and stood at the junction of Boundary Road and Hardres Street.

Towns produced their own gas by baking coal in huge sealed ovens. The heat drove off the gas which was then stored in vast tanks that we called gasometers, these in turn fed the underground pipework to everyone's home. The other principle by-products of the coal were coke and tar. The gasometers are still around but now contain natural gas from the oil fields. Coke was a valuable slow burning boiler fuel and most houses had a boiler to heat the kitchen or living room and provide hot water. Bill Matthews, a part time fireman in my father's Southwood sub-station, delivered a hundredweight of coke and a hundredweight of coal almost every week in winter. Maybe less coke and no coal in the summer months. He still delivered by horse and cart. Outside many houses with cellars was a round cast iron lid about 15 inches in diameter set into the pavement or garden path, it had a shoot below it that led on down to the house's cellar. The coke had to be carried down through the house to avoid mixing the two fuels but as it was nowhere near so dirty and dusty as coal that did not matter. Those without cellars had a coal bunker in the back garden or shed. Rural areas lacked gas but used wood, paraffin or oil burning cookers; also for central heating as its use spread during the 60s and 70s. I joined the central heating world in 1969 after converting a terrace of four tiny, derelict cottages into a house. What a delight after six months in a frozen caravan with two young children.

When the war ended street lighting, as before, was by gas lamps which gave a soft yellowish light and were switched on and off by hand-wound time clocks that had replaced the lamplighter men of my father's youth. There were still many houses lit solely by gas and the gas companies had a hundred year contract with the railway to provide the lighting on their premises; this still had years to run.

Rationing continued

My Saturday routine immediately after breakfast was to cycle down to Darby's, the pork butcher in the High Street, then wait in a hundred yard queue for two hours or more for our weeks supply of chipolatas or sausages. In wet weather this was not a lot of fun. My father was a creature of habit. He loved his Sunday morning breakfast, half a grapefruit, (during that period he had to forego the grapefruit unless he could get the tinned version,) then a few pork chipolatas followed by toast and marmalade and two cups of tea. He would often say to my mother: "Have I had my second cup?" If she said "Yes" that was it, he never asked for a third. His lunch each day was almost invariably followed by stewed fruit and Bird's custard. Supper was an apple and two slices of Ryvita with factory Cheddar cheese. Very monotonous but it kept him quite content.

The war lasted six years but rationing lasted fourteen. Queuing was a large part of all shoppers' time. There was also a black market with which my father would have no association. He despised those who did. I recall waiting in line just beside the till inside a local grocers. A customer paused to pay on his way out and I saw the owner slide a packet from below the bacon machine and pass it discreetly across with the change and a quick wink. I'm sure it went on all the time. Bacon allowance was just 4oz per week. Those caught were severely punished, so I expect the profits on such deals were high. Shortages were still acute. In 1946 bread, exempt during the war, was put on ration until 1948. It was not until six years later, in 1954, that meat and fats were finally de-rationed and bananas ceased to be rationed later the same year.

Eleven Plus

I and my fellow scholars were prepared for the Eleven Plus examination. Mr Stanley teaching us for a second year maintained the brilliant record set up by his predecessor, "Tiddly", who had suddenly retired. He reproduced endless copies of old Eleven Plus exam papers on a machine called a cyclostyle. The copies were about the quality of those from a typewriter duplicate but using badly worn mauve carbon paper, but by the time we took the exam we were very familiar with the type of question we would face on the day. Sixteen pupils passed in my year, a far greater proportion than any of the other schools in Thanet. Vast comprehensive or technical schools did not exist until the 60s.

There were losers. Sadly, the boy who sat next to me was nervous during the exam and failed although he was normally very near the top of the class and should have easily passed. This was a great shame. Some people do badly under time pressure. When given more time and no pressure they may be better than those who excel in exams. There was no official recognition of dyslexia then, nor for another forty years so many children missed out. Now many dyslexics get through university. The same should be true for deaf children, in the 60s there was only one specialist grammar school for the 23,600 deaf children in the UK, approximately 1,700 in each academic year. Privately owned, it had places for 60 children each year paid for by their local authority. More than half went on to university, a great credit to the Mary Hare Grammar School. What about the chances of the remaining 1,640 who did not have this opportunity? There are those would say "Shut the school, it gives some children an unfair advantage" instead of thinking "How can we go on failing these kids." It was scandalous. When I was a child deaf children used to be thought of as deaf and dumb. Children must be taught to lipread and read before they can learn to talk. Sign language is for the most severely handicapped, but it isolates them from the bulk of people. Great advances were made from the 60s onward, not only with teaching methods. There was an increase in those taught lipreading and huge technical improvement in hearing aids. There are many differently handicapped children who still miss out. I only have detailed knowledge of the two mentioned as I have had a child in each group. Both went to university after struggling through the education system. I have every sympathy with immigrant children's education but surely we have at very least as much responsibility for all our own who did not choose their handicap.

124

Holiday jobs

During one summer holiday Brian and I built a go-cart from the wheels and axles of a derelict pram, 5 bolts, a wooden box, a piece board and a length of cord and set up a very short term business tracking down delivery horses whose droppings we later sold to his grandfather and a friend of my grandfather for their roses.

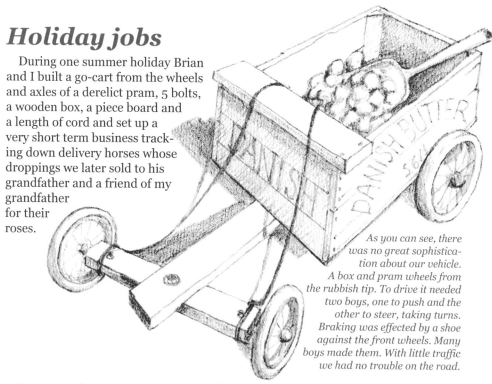

As you can see, there was no great sophistication about our vehicle. A box and pram wheels from the rubbish tip. To drive it needed two boys, one to push and the other to steer, taking turns. Braking was effected by a shoe against the front wheels. Many boys made them. With little traffic we had no trouble on the road.

To earn pocket money during the holidays I was now just about big enough to act as a van boy, aiding one of my grandfather's delivery drivers by getting goods to the back of the Bedford van for him. Although the main business was supplying bakers with everything except their flour, Grandpa had for many years supplemented it as an agent for Suttons, a firm of carriers. I am not sure if they undertook deliveries nationwide or not but our company covered Kent for them. Once a week we delivered out as far as Tunbridge Wells and the mid Kent villages so that my geography of Kent was fairly good long before I took my driving test.

With comparatively little traffic on the roads in those days George Homersham, the driver for this long delivery round, would let me lean over and steer the vehicle and change gear on the long straight stretches. One day, occupied like this and approaching Chilham the front wheel suddenly either collapsed or came off. I'm not sure which but we certainly stopped rather fast, lucky to not end up in the ditch. At that time 45 mph was quite a good speed for vans. The war had put road maintenance on a back boiler, they were much more bumpy and the bends far sharper and more frequent than now because this had never been a problem for horse drawn traffic. Indeed smooth roads could prove a problem for horses by giving insufficient grip. Very steep hills sometimes had a surface with lines of granite sets alternating with wood blocks to aid the animals grip. There were still no motorways.

When the day was over I used to make sure my father was busy elsewhere when I went to the office to collect my pay. My father would give me a shilling, 5p, but Grandpa was good for half a crown. Twelve and a half metric pence.

Wolf Cubs and Scouts

Organisations joined by young people included the Scouting movement and the Boys Brigade. I think the Boys Brigade was more popular among those of a musical bent as it had a band. Between nine and eleven I was in the 5th Ramsgate Wolf Cubs, I enrolled and was then entitled to wear small green tags attached to the elastic garters that we used to hold up our socks. Remember we all wore shorts up to the age of about thirteen. The things I learnt there have proved useful. Various knots, the flags of different countries, also how to make camp fires and burn sausages to death on them in a billycan. At eleven I became the Senior Sixer, the ultimate rank in the Cubs, and I left. I failed to join the Scouts as homework at grammar school left very little time for such occupations. I wanted spare time for other interests.

About the age of eleven I became very interested in model making and built model sailing ships of matchsticks stuck together with balsa cement and rigged with human hair and later with split hair. This interest led me to join Ramsgate Model Club which met in a bomb damaged building at the end of Princes Street and had some quite sophisticated equipment. Most of the members were adult, some very skilled at making steam engines of various sizes and steam operated pumps. I felt rather out of place, but they were very kind and allowed me to use a lathe to make small brass cannons for a larger model galleon. This period was short lived, probably because I had difficulty fitting in an evening with so much homework.

Later I made this 7cm high model for my mother. The hull is wood with thin sheet pewter super-structure and is rigged with split human hair. The sea is a mixture of blue and green sealing wax.

In some ways I feel very sorry for children today. Much of the satisfaction we had in the past was in creating our own things, bikes built from parts of older bikes, bits swapped between friends, bits bought over months from limited pocket money. Now bikes, motorbikes, cars or boats are expected to be made of high tech materials of the latest design. Christmas or birthday presents not just a book, something in shiny chrome or stainless steel or fibreglass. The latest computer or games machine. Their expectations are of a finished product that will be the envy of their contemporaries; luxuries undreamed of by their grandparents. At Chatham House, the headmaster and a couple of senior masters had cars. When I last visited the school, still a State owned, it looked as if the entire sixth form had cars, not old bangers either; nice, roadworthy cars.

126

Grammar school

My father had been a pupil at Chatham House *(as had Isambard Brunel the great Victorian engineer and later, Prime Minister, the Rt. Hon. Sir Edward Heath, KG., MBE.)* I have my father's school reports and that he had been an outstanding pupil both academically and on the sports field is clear from reading them. A number of the older masters had formerly taught him and for some strange reason assumed I would be similarly gifted. They were to be sadly disillusioned. Each year was split into three forms, forms, A, B and C. I was allocated

Chatham House Grammar School
1797-1997

to C and stayed there for the rest of my school career. I was unable to get to grips with algebra, theorems, or the science subjects, was hopeless at French and suspect many of my fellow pupils, shining in that subject, never spent more than a few weeks in France. Most people only require another language for verbal communication. Keep it simple and teach it early: past historic or subjuctive clauses are for those wishing to specialise. Give pupils a feeling of instant success. After all, I go now/I go yesterday/I go tomorrow are all understandable. Tell them any French word ending in *"tion"* is the same as English with only two exceptions and they suddenly have a vocabulary of over two thousand words. Make it fun. I have lived extensively in Europe and two Middle Eastern countries and found the rest much easier learnt on site.

I was similarly a failure on the sports field having very little interest in throwing myself wholeheartedly onto the frozen mud of a January rugby field on Saturday mornings. I have to confess that this failure to perform was, in part, deliberate. School five days a week was reasonable, but losing even a moment of the weekend was totally unacceptable when I had so many other interesting things to do.

Cricket had the same appeal for me. Standing for hours on end at the boundary of the cricket pitch dressed in glorious whites, my first long trousers, waiting for some bright spark to waft the ball in my direction had a dramatic lack of appeal. I developed an instant hatred for boxing when, in the first minute of my one and only boxing match, my opponent whacked me in the solar plexus completely winding me and putting me off this violent sport for all time. Swimming and lifesaving did take my fancy and were taught by the art master. I was able to skive off cricket and athletics to enjoy these options.

There were luckily incidents which enlivened the day. For example in my second year a young chemistry master joined the school. Doubtless very knowledgeable or he would have never gained a place on the staff. Being clever is unfortunately not the end of teaching. The guy had no idea how to control a class. You may have conducted an experiment while of similar tender age where an inverted tin about the size of a baked bean can is partly filled with gas which is then lit and explodes up into the air. Our explosions were aimed, unsuccessfully, to break the light bulbs. On a hot day the poor idiot opened the lab door which gave onto the lower playground. As it had a tendency to swing shut he propped it open with a fire extinguisher, one of the old carrot shaped units with a striker knob on top; of course we knew exactly how to play this one. Notes passed between us below lab bench level. As the closing bell sounded there was a rush for the door, the first boy accidentally knocking over the extinguisher, the next accidentally kicking in the striker knob while others orientated it back toward the master's end of the room in their scramble to leave the class. We then all rolled around laughing while "Sir" struggled to get the thing out into the yard, soaking himself in the process.

The lower corridor of the main building passes the Head's study and at the southern end has stairs down to what in my time was the locker room. No running in corridors and walk properly down stairs. The games master, Mr Mahony was a decent chap and did a great deal to raise the standard of sport in the school. Late for my next class I hared along the corridor and jumped the short staircase. While I was in mid flight, like Harry Potter without his broom, Mr Mahony stepped round the corner and I landed smack on his foot. My heart stopped, I was viewing instant death, thirty times round the top field with no stopping, detentions for life, straight to the Head for a whacking. The angels were on my side. "Sorry boy, didn't see you" and off he went up the stairs. At that time headmasters could cane pupils; even prefects could give up to twelve whacks with a plimsoll if a boy was found guilty by the prefects court of breaking a school rule.

There was a different outcome to another event. The senior English master was horrid little man who had also taught my father. Looking over your shoulder as you worked and seeing an error would twist your ear hard or smack you across the knuckles with the edge his ruler. As I said, he was a little man and on this day he made a serious mistake. Once to often he whacked the knuckles of a mild but powerful six footer who was doing his best. We shall call him Smith. Smith rocketed to his feet, picked up "Sir" by the shoulders, clean off the floor and rapped him sharply against the wall three times before dropping him semi-conscious on the floor. Then Smith left the room and was never seen at school again. Of course expelled, but in the opinion of the entire class the wrong person got the chop. That master had been abusing his position for generations.

Not all subjects defeated me. I did fairly well in English and history although the history master, another of those who had taught my father, marked me down in the class. He said I didn't deserve the marks I got because in his opinion I did not make sufficient effort. My forte lay in art, woodwork and technical drawing in which I was able to come top or second in the class for most of the time. I owe a great deal to the two masters who taught me those subjects as they have been of great benefit and pleasure to me throughout my life and am therefore enormously grateful to the school.

Mr Lamb, the art master who later became a headmaster, really taught art. How to use perspective before moving on to anything else. It amazes me how few children have that benefit today. He also invited those of us who were interested to his flat to make recorders from vulcanite tube and then formed a recorder club for us. He was a great help to me. Art had been one of my major interests since the present of my watercolour set when much younger. Each year the school put on a play, helping to paint the scenery was another opportunity for me to legitimately escape games. Technical drawing and woodwork were taught by Mr Weeks, another patient, kindly man to whom I owe a great deal. These allied subjects, have both proved vastly useful to me over the years. Perhaps less useful was an early lesson on how to heat wood glue, then the only wood glue, a product used for centuries was derived from animal hooves. It was necessary to heat it gently and use it hot. This was done in a container surrounded by water, rather like the way mothers' cook Christmas puddings. Joints were glued and had to be clamped for several days to ensure a sound joint. Now the choice of adhesives is vast and setting time greatly reduced or instantaneous.

Holidays started again

With a gradual return to normality, the removal of restrictions on travel and close to full employment, people's minds turned to holidays. The working week was 48 hours which did not leave a great deal of time for relaxation. Holidays were commonly only one or two weeks a year. Folk owning their own home often spent one week of the break redecorating, the second week would give the chance of a holiday away. The traditional holiday resorts started to boom. Holidays abroad had yet to arrive, because, as we have seen, Europe was in chaos. Coastal places like Blackpool, Southend, Ramsgate and Brighton started to pick up.

The old paddle steamers got a new lease of life plying from London down to Southend and Margate. Day trippers piled onto the weekend steam trains and an almost endless column of charabancs (coaches to you) arrived at the coastal resorts delivering visitors on their firms annual outing with two or three barrels of beer in the luggage compartment, half dry before they even arrived at their destination. Saturdays saw dozens of coaches with the holidaymakers for the coming week arriving all morning and then departing later with those whose vacation had just finished. The streets of Ramsgate became clogged with lobster coloured Londoners, the women with "Kiss me quick" hats and the men with large handkerchiefs knotted at each corner balanced on their shining red bald heads. Cycling to school became hazardous as they were all over the road, oblivious to traffic, frequently oblivious to everything if the truth be told. You may have seen their children or grandchildren while on holiday in coastal Spain.

I think some of the old paddle steamers had been sunk while commandeered by the Navy for war work. The survivors were quickly refurbished to give London holiday trippers a pleasant day out in Southend or Margate. Others ferried their passengers to the Channel Isles, France and the Isle of Wight.

Cattle were still being driven on foot from local farms into town to the slaughterhouse at the top of Pig Alley, off the High Street. This added to the general congestion. Lorries were generally to small to carry many animals, so it made sense to walk them in, in bulk, as in centuries past. Once the slaughterhouse man had shut the doors we boys leaned our bikes against them and tried to climb on them high enough to see what happened next. Our gruesome interest was frustrated. As the frightened mooing decreased we failed to get a view of anything except the feet of the carcasses as they hung from a rail fixed to the ceiling. The doors were too high.

We had had the benefit of several holidays with our cousins and both sets of grandparents during school breaks. In 1947 we went on a real holiday travelling in my grandfather's venerable car, a real holiday, in a boarding house, in Wadhurst, leaving behind my new post-war brother in the care of an aunt. We revisited nearby Lamberhurst and Mrs Chandler whose husband had died, Jimmy Haskell's mum and several relations. We saw museums, castles and ancient churches, their churchyards containing great, crooked tombstones with the gruesome skull and crossbones and barely legible names and ancient yew trees left over from the times of the druids. On to Brighton and Hove, the childhood home of my mother. We had lunch with "Auntie" Nancy, she of the half crown fame. *(p34)* We also toured to Penshurst Place and Hastings Castle where I believe I first saw line portraits by Holbien. They were simple line drawings of groups of people, with no apparent rubbing out. Spot on likenesses first time, I just stared and stared, amazed at his skill. I still stare, jealous and amazed.

During this one and only holiday I ever shared with my parents I was given the princely sum of five shillings (25p) to spend as I wished. After wasting hours of the family's time I finally chose two tennis balls. I had never previously seen new balls and it was a long time before I used them. On the way home the car began to give trouble with a slipping clutch. My father said it had been made by Rolls Canardley. Rolls down the hill but can 'ardly get up the next. It was actually a Vauxhall made about 1932 but had been on holiday for lack of fuel throughout the war years.

There were two other notable, non church outings with my parents. In 1946 they took me to London to see the Crazy Gang's long running show at the Victoria Palace. I have since gained the impression that my father rather regretted his choice as the jokes, in the true tradition of English variety shows, were fairly risque. He need not have worried, they went clean over my young head and I was not at all clear about why the rest of the audience were laughing until hearing excerpts some years later on the radio. The following year we returned to London, this time to the Coliseum to see Dolores Gray in "Annie get your gun". A great and memorable success that ran for two years and was seen by over two and a half million people. Of course locally there were variety concerts, Seaside Showboat and Ice Shows to entertain the visitors during the summer season and plays at the local theatres.

Please don't get the idea we had no family outings. Until old enough to find our own amusements, Saturday afternoons and national holidays were great family affairs. We went for long walks, spent afternoons having picnics in the country and touring ancient, historic, or otherwise interesting places, or visiting relations, in post-war years often in company with Mother's sister's family, newly returned from India and pictured below.

A 1956 family picnic in a corn field. As I am the only one not pictured I assume that I was the photographer.

Note the stooks of corn that, ten years after the war ended, were still harvested using a reaper and binder.

131

Manual labour

Most sacked products today come in bags not exceeding 25kg. They arrive in a juggernaught carrying its own forklift or lorry-mounted crane. They are packed on pallets and off-loaded onto pallet trucks. In my youth none of these existed, there were no limits to the weight people were expected to handle. One hundredweight, (about 50 kilos) was the standard sack for coal, sugar, salt etc. We had salt delivered by rail and had to collect it from a goods wagon in the railway yard. Many products were loose packed in hessian sacks which provided a good grip. Salt, being very small grains, arrived in cotton sacks that started as 1cwt but absorbed huge amounts of water, then set like concrete often in incredibly awkward shapes. When I helped unload a couple of tons of it from a goods wagon the sacks could be getting towards double their dry weight and set solid. It was no use complaining about it. That just proved you were a wimp.

If goods were to be stocked above the ground floor level they were hoisted by a rope over a pulley wheel or with a time consuming chain lift, or frequently on the ware-houseman's shoulders. Small businesses seldom had a three phase electric supply and single phase electric hoists were not available until the late 1960s when I started selling one made by GIS Hoists in Switzerland. The days of exploiting child labour were over but plenty of very hard manual work remained. Mechanised handling of products, apart from roller conveyors had yet to be introduced.

After WW1 the world had suffered a huge depression and many people had been out of work. Following WW2 men were for the moment content to be in work instead of fighting. Dockers were expected to carry more than their own weight out of ships; bummarees, the porters in the Smithfield meat market, walked around with huge weights of frozen cow on their shoulder and back injuries were common. Nowadays workmen are protected from these problems by regulations, although nurses seem to have been discreetly bypassed. The regulations exist, but human suffering overrules it for a nurse.

The National Health Service instructs them never, on any account, to lift someone who is too heavy for them knowing full well that a caring nurse will always rush to assist a patient who has fallen or had a mishap. If the nurse then suffers a strain they can sit on their hands and say: "She was told never to do that" and refuse to pay compensation. To replace the injured nurse the NHS will then resort to an agency nurse, pay her much more than their own staff, plus substantial commission to the agency. Chances are this replacement nurse will come from another country and fail to communicate with the patients because neither understands the other's accent.

When I first started in business I had to supplement my meagre income by each evening loading local farm produce onto lorries for the old, now defunct, Covent Garden or Borough Markets in London. Usually cabbage, or sprouts, in winter and fruit in summer. Occasionally the product was wheat or barley in sacks of between two-and-a-quarter and two-and-a-half hundredweight *(approximately 112-125kg)*. Each sack was put on a wind-up hoist to lift the top of the sack to shoulder height and off I wobbled. I can tell you my legs felt like old rhubarb by the time the lorry was loaded.

Not all workers were happy with the new regulations:

BY IAN MURRAY... The Times: 21 June 1996.

A £2 million "redundancy" package yesterday brought down one of the last bastions of trade union restrictive practices. Smithfield meat market in London. A total of 162 porters,
69 of them pensioners and many more than 70 years old, had been holding out against the introduction of equipment to carry carcasses required by the European Union.

The porters, self employed and consequently not entitled to redundancy, are all members of the Transport and General Workers Union. They are allowed to work in the market under a licence granted by the Corporation of London. Only those nominated by the union are given a licence and they guard their closed shop closely. Queen Elizabeth the Queen Mother is an honorary member.

The porters, who are divided into specialist groups of pullers-back, pitchers, shunters, cartminders and bummarees, have been handling meat the same way as their Victorian forefathers. The pullers-back drag the carcasses to the tailboard of the incoming vehicles. The pitchers carry goods from the tailboards and pitch them into the market. The shunters move the lorries and the bummarees have the exclusive right to carry the meat from the market to the buyer's vehicle. They are paid a penny for each pound of meat they shift and, with 2,500 tonnes of meat going through the market each week, can earn up to £50,000 a year.

EU regulations came into force three years ago requiring all meat to be handled mechanically and forbidding porters from tossing carcasses over their shoulders or onto trolleys. The Corporation, which owns the markets and has a statutory duty to provide them, launched a £60 million refurbishment of the Grade II listed Victorian halls, equipping them with overhead rails to transport carcasses. Although work on the first hall was completed last year, it is still not in use because of the difficulty in making the porters accept that they are redundant.

The Corporation recruited Dennis Boyd, chief reconciliation officer at ACAS for 12 years, had 59 meetings with the porters and the Smithfield Market Traders Association over two years and said it was the most complicated negotiation with which he had been involved. As recently as last month he had made little progress.

In the end he advised the Corporation to pay redundancy money even though the porters were not entitled to it. Even those over retirement age were offered £8,000each. Others would receive up to £20,000. About 30 bummarees who will run the overhead system will keep their jobs. The traders, anxious to move into the refurbished hall, agreed to pay 40% of the bill. A final meeting with the pitchers at 4am yesterday clinched the deal.

Reading and the Public Library

Like most young boys I liked comics, "Chicks Own" mentioned earlier was the beginning. It was followed by "Dandy" and "Beano" both of them still available, "Radio Fun", "Hotspur" and "Eagle". Without a shadow of doubt "Eagle", a late arrival, was the best for the ten to thirteen age group. It was better printed than its competitors and cleverly mixed fact and science fiction. One day riding home with it spread across my handlebars, I ran smack into the back of a parked furniture lorry. Hearing about it my father said: "I don't know why you read that stuff, people won't be going to the moon in your lifetime". I designed a rocket to take me there, but lacked the resources to build it so the American's beat me too it. In fact my Grandma Cain, born in 1874, almost twenty years before the first cars came on the scene, lived to be a hundred and three and watched the first moon landing, live, on television in 1969.

I have always been a bit of a bookworm and many were the torch batteries that died under my bed covers after the light had been put out by my mother or father with the injunction: "Go to sleep now". From the age of seven, or eight, I read the multitude of books from the pen of Enid Blyton, quite the most prolific children's writer of the 40s and 50s. Then came books that my father had as a child; nationalistic and Empire proud, mostly written during or just after the first World War and filled with stories of heroism and the horrors of the trench warfare, barbed wire and no-man's land, or adventures and battles against wild tribes in the Middle East. Descriptions of early aviators escaping from desert kingdoms. The journeys across Africa of Dr Livingstone. Then the Biggles series of a pilot's adventures set in World War II. Following these came classics from the 1800s such as the Waverley Novels and The Scarlet Pimpernel from my Grandpa Cain's collection. Later the Romany series on natural history by the Romany gypsy writer and broadcaster Rev George Bramwell Evans.

The local librarian, a wise man, had a rule that children could have three tickets entitling them to borrow three books at any one time. Two for fiction, but the third had to be non-fiction. I averaged about five books a week. As a result of this rule I also read about construction of boats and aircraft, crafts, art and travel and anything else I could get my hands on. You will probably note that none of these seem to fit into a school curriculum. Maths and Shakespeare were not included.

Like many of my age, books provided the escape that present day youngsters get from television or games machines, or by endless hours on mobile phones. The added benefit for my age group was that we used our imagination to paint the scenes in our head instead of having a games designer do it for us. If you don't read books, try it. It is painless and can be done at a moments notice and no need to recharge a battery unless of course you are also doing it under the bedclothes.

Church activities

In common with vast sections of the population my family attended chapel or church each Sunday. Churches were pretty full during the war and the immediate post-war years. Women without contact from sons or husbands for months on end, not knowing where in the world they were fighting, fearing they were injured or dead, looked for reassurance. Service personel from far afield but stationed locally or on leave from battlefields went seeking a break from their horrors and stress and found churches gave a little peace, hope and comfort. They also provided many activities and involved far more people, both young and old, than is the case nowadays. Several churches had been bombed. The Methodist Chapel had been totally destroyed, consequently services were held in the Centenary Hall further up the street. Tuesday evening was Guild night attended by young adults, married people and those of more mature years, but occasionally a special event was open to interested older children as well. Speakers were invited from all walks of life and I particularly recall a lecture and slide show given by the missionary, Mildred Cable, who had five times crossed the vast Gobi Desert in company with two sisters, Eva and Francesca French. These middle aged, indomitable women had travelled with a donkey to distribute Bibles to the inhabitants and were the first Europeans ever to undertake the hazards of Chinese warlords and dust storms to traverse the Gobi, one of the largest deserts in the world and mostly rock. This may seem pretty tame stuff now, but at the time few people in the audience had crossed the Channel, never seen an Indian, or Jamaican, never mind wild tribesmen with Mongolian features. Newspapers of the period had few pages, paper was in short supply and reproduction of pictures by letterpress printing was expensive.

Precursors of the cinema, lantern shows were still quite common. The projector had an electric bulb or powerful carbon arc lamp and the glass slides were of black and white photos, some hand coloured and frequently somewhat the worse for wear. For all that, very interesting, seeing and hearing firsthand the adventures of these women and the scenes and people they had encountered on their considerable journeys. In those less sophisticated times, when television had yet to take over the livingroom, much of the world was still unmapped and unphotographed and only seen by this method or taking the National Geographical magazine. It was in one of these that I first saw pictures of half naked women in Bahli, indeed looking for more of these fascinations was probably what drove me to continue research of this excellent publication. Nudity had no place in newspapers or regular magazines and was regarded as something rather shocking.

Wednesday was youth club when we younger members of the church could meet to play table tennis, play records, indoor hockey or rehearse the Christmas nativity play. Each year there were joint events with other clubs. Arts festivals for solos, vocal or instrumental, choirs, duets and various crafts held either in Canterbury, or Chatham. I was lucky enough to win several times in the drawing or painting competitions and as a spin-off started producing hand painted Christmas cards which I sold to kindly adults.

Thursday was the Women's Bright Hour. As I was never a member I can tell you nothing about it except that it was mostly attended by the older women. Friday was Choir Practice. Saturdays were reserved for our annual sports day, jumble sales and the Sunday School Outing. Also from time to time there was a rally when all the local Methodist churches joined together to hear a well known speaker, always a Church Minister. This was normally followed by a meal or afternoon tea. Of course the highlight of the week was Sunday when there were services in the morning and evening with Sunday School in the afternoon.

My father was the Sunday School Superintendent for 30 years, a member of the choir and a Trustee, one of the chapel administrators. He also helped run the Youth Club, so I was inevitably involved, quite willingly when young and increasingly resentfully when older. I hasten to add that, apart from coercing me into taking part, neither he nor my mother gave me the least reason to doubt their sincerity. I was taught to say my prayers at three-years-old before sleeping, kneeling beside my bed, and have an early memory of seeing through the partly open door of my parents' bedroom, their feet in a position which clearly indicated they were kneeling together beside their bed doing the same thing. I never heard either of them speaking loudly or unpleasantly to one another and can only recall one occasion when my mother said "Oh Douglas" in an exasperated voice to my father. His honesty was commented on to me later in life by trades people who dealt all their business lives with him because of it.

In one respect he was bigoted as were many in the UK and throughout Europe. While being in no way a supporter of active anti-Semitism he regarded the Jews with a degree of suspicion even though his grandmother was a half-Polish Jewess. There were several who attended our church of whom he would say: "They are Jewish, but have become Christians now". Apparently that made them respectable in his eyes. I asked him about his attitude one day and he told me Jews had, in his opinion, disgraced themselves in the business world, they would seek to get out of verbal contracts if it suited them, whereas British businessmen would normally stand by their word. It seems strange in present times as now most have followed their lead. In the end it was my brother's dealing with Jewish hotels that reversed his opinion. A Jewish owned hotel went bankrupt, but the surrounding Jewish hoteliers paid his debts, enhancing their good name in the community. This was not an example ever followed by neighbouring British organisations. I find nothing divides the world more than mindless religious prejudice.

136

Music lessons

My father played the piano and also the Church organ if the organist was away. He was determined I should learn. As result I had to go once a week to a middle-aged lady who lived with her mother. The elderly mother painted in oil colours, each week another forest glade with spring trees and bluebells, indistinguishable from the last. Both were pleasant people and I was not at all averse to learning, but unfortunately they had two elderly spaniels. Those dogs stank, not just slightly unwashed. More like dogs rolled in long dead hedgehog if you have ever had that rich experience. The smell reached almost the length of the garden path and after about six months I decided I could no longer put up with it. By that time I was able to play a piece called "The Teddy Bears' picnic". Not discouraged, my father demanded which of the remaining instruments in the house I would like to play. "I'd like to learn the clarinet, it's great for traditional jazz and for orchestral pieces". Father was no jazz fan and knew I had only introduced the mention of orchestral pieces as bait, but knew it had no chance. The choice was actually between a trombone and my aunt's old 'cello. I plumped for the latter and received lessons from Mr Price who also taught, or rather failed, to teach me French. It went quite well, I became a member of the school orchestra and on one occasion played with a local amateur orchestra. After leaving school I had lessons from the first woman to ever play with the London Philharmonic Orchestra. She was very good and I used to arrive early just to stand outside her window and listen to her playing to amuse herself. Later, what with homework, sailing and finding some-thing living with a shape vaguely reminiscent of the 'cello I stopped. Many years later I bought a clarinet but never became proficient.

My aunt, a registered Nanny, in the uniform she was required to wear when on duty in the house.

Domestic service

The disparity between rich and poor was greater before the war and gave considerable employment to domestic staff. Even middle class families could often afford to have help, either a live in housemaid or a "Mrs Mopp" to do the floor cleaning and help with the housework. This was particularly useful for the elderly or infirm, also for mothers with new babies. The extra washing coupled with broken nights was eased by having someone to do the ironing The wealthy employed Nannies to care for their offspring leaving them free for business or

Centre below: Airing her charge in company with other nannies.

138

social affairs, and still do so. Learning to be a nannie was regarded as excellent training for a girl as she would be well able to look after her own children in due course. A trained nanny ruled her charge's life. Told parents when it would be convenient for them to see their children, could forbid them to wake the child when it slept. Said what time it should sleep, what it should eat and often was in charge of a nursery nurse to do the washing of the child's clothes and nappies and keep the nursery area clean and tidy.

Remember that prior to the war most women did not work. Those with a low income could supplement it by doing a bit of charring. Charladies cleaned the office blocks or "did" for somebody. In 1946 when my mother found herself overstretched looking after my youngest brother who had a heart problem, she asked around and found a neighbour who "did" for several other families in the area and agreed to "do" for us twice a week. She undertook the scrubbing of the kitchen floor and helped with the ironing and polished the floor lino in the passageways. We were still some years away from automatic washing machines.

Except for a mat in front of the sink to keep feet warmer, sculleries' floors were bare tile or cement. Kitchens usually had lino as we called linoleum, often cheered up with a rug. These floors needed regular scrubbing. Throughout the rest of the ground floor the wood planking was stained dark brown or covered with lino on top of which unfitted carpets were usually laid. Most people had carpet runners laid down the middle of the passages and on stairs where it was held in place with brass or wooden stair rods. Lino and woodwork needed wax polishing and, like the kitchen floors, was a down on your knees job and rub, rub, rub. Not a quick swish over with the vacuum cleaner. Bedroom floors were often left plain with a rug or covering of a cheaper product called Congoleum which had a printed design on it.

Gamages was a major London store from the late 1800s to 1972 and sold just about everything. This is from their 1936 catalogue.

139

The heavy Death Duty tax imposed by the immediate post-war Government led to the closure of a lot of stately homes and estates which had been in the care of the same family for generations. Staff, many of whom had worked for the estate all their lives, found themselves homeless or allocated a council house but without work. Buyers were rare. Sometimes the local authority took over the buildings as extra offices, frequently butchering the interiors in the process. Listed building protection did not come into proper force until the 1950s. Later when councils expanded they built new offices and unable to afford the cost of upkeep had the stately mansions bulldozed into the ground.

With increasing mechanisation in homes there was less need for Mrs Mops. People started to advertise for au pairs to assist them. The idea was that an au pair lived as a working guest to help her learn the language. Unfortunately they were frequently seen as little more than slave labour. Contract office cleaning companies were formed and took over from the individual charladies. Now it is very difficult to find domestic help and those doing the job are in a strong position when it comes to negotiating payment.

Parades, fetes, Remembrance Day

After the war, nationwide, there were frequent parades. In Ramsgate this was mostly during the summer where they provided an attraction for the vast number of visitors who swarmed into the resort; also on Armistice Sunday celebrated in November. The various denominations held their morning services then all parties assembled to hold a parade. Taking part would be the Salvation Army, a military band, often the Royal Marines from their School of Music in Deal and a contingent of American airmen from Manston who slouched by chewing their gum in marked contrast to the Marines. On Armistice Sunday the newly elected mayor, glorious in his gold chain, together with the scarlet robed aldermen and the town's councillors in blue, joined in the parade along with ex servicemen, now in civilian clothes but wearing all their medals. There were Scouts, the Boys' Brigade and the Air Force bands and representatives of other organisations including St John's Ambulance Brigade. Drum majors leading the bands were an important part of the spectacle vying with one another to throw their maces ever higher into the air and deftly catching them again as they marched. The St John's Ambulance drum major, Eric Easton, was by far the most spectacular.

The local parades were never complete without "Donkey". Donkey was a man with a slight mental problem but happy, friendly and completely harmless. He adored processions of any kind and like a jester capered along at the head of the column enjoying the cheering of the crowd. All the locals knew him and I cannot recall any occasion when he was restrained from taking part, indeed when he finally failed to appear one year everyone was asking what had happened to him.

For several years after the war there were regular fetes in the park with stalls such as guess the weight of the pig, coconut shies, etc. These affairs were popular with the boys as they attracted a lot of foreign students so we had a chance to chat up the girls. The whole thing ended with a fireworks display, the girls pretending fright with the bangs needed protective arms round them; out of sight of the family who had care of them. In the crush of spectators and darkness hands could wander and kisses be exchanged.

140

The Harbour

In the years immediately after the war there were no luxury yachts in Ramsgate harbour, in fact very few boats of any sort. About once a fortnight a beautiful flat bottomed Thames spritsail barge owned by Everards came in with grain for Hudson's flour mill. Capable of carrying up to 250 tons with a sail area of up to 5,000 sq ft (460 sq metres) they were the largest working sailing ships handled by only two men. Coasters imported wood for the local timber yard at the top of the High Street and two converted motor torpedo boats took holidaymakers for trips round the Goodwin Sands. I took the trip on one but the motion was very different from that of a small dinghy. After about ten minutes I locked myself in the toilet and stayed there for the next two hours clutching my stomach and head in turns to the distress of the rest of the passengers. A strange thing, seasickness, once back on dry land I went immediately for fish and chips.

There were a few boats docked by their owners at the start of the war and never reclaimed. Probably the owners had died either of old age or from the results of war. There were also four or five working trawlers. My father told me that in his youth it had been possible to walk clean across the inner harbour on the decks of the trawlers when they all returned to port for Christmas.

Goodbye to warrior of the storms

VETERAN of the tough days of Ramsgate Harbour at the turn of the century and a crew member of the lifeboat for 45 years, Mr. Henry John Verrion died in hospital last week at the age of 91.

Mr. Verrion was born at Ramsgate. His family were of French extraction and had moved to Thanet from Cornwall. He attended Christ Church School and at an early age began his lifetime's work at the Harbour.

His long career at the Harbour was varied. He fished, ran pleasure trips and worked on a variety of cargo vessels. He owned several boats himself, including Our Boys, Indian Chief, Blossom, Sir Charles Warren, Skylark, Swift, Anna and Clara Bell.

Mr. Verrion began his long association with the lifeboat at the age of 20, when lifeboats put to sea under sail.

One of his outstanding lifeboat adventures was in 1919, when he helped in the rescue of 30 survivors of the American vessel Piave, which went down on the Goodwin Sands. He was presented with a gold medal from the President of the United States and it remained one of his proudest possessions.

During World War I, Mr. Verrion was also a watchman on the East Pierhead.

Mr. Verrion was a Forester all his life. He leaves three sons, one of whom, Mr. Arthur Verrion, is now coxwain of Ramsgate Lifeboat. He lived with another son, Herbert, and his daughter-in-law, at 139 Boundary-road.

The funeral took place at Ramsgate Cemetery yesterday (Tuesday).

Mr Verrion who taught me to row and to scull with one oar.

The outer harbour was where I learnt to row before having my boat. I hired a small dinghy from an old fisherman, Mr Verrion. A very kindly old gentleman who sometimes let me borrow his boat for nothing, he was in his eighties but could still swarm up a rope to get back onto the fish market slipway. Worried about the possibility of him falling I once asked if he could swim well. He replied that he had never learnt, in common with many others brought up in the age of square rigged ships. It took so long to turn one that a man overboard was as good as dead, swimming just prolonged the agony.

141

A THAMES BARGE

These were the last working sailing ships used round the coast of Britain and I often passed one as a boy in my dinghy off Ramsgate. Fully loaded and with their lee deck awash they sailed more slowly than a dinghy but could point up into the wind extremely well and were a beautiful sight. Built as pure sailing vessels most were fitted with an auxilliary engine during the 1930s for manoeuvring in port. The last survivors retired in the early 1970s to become privately owned, many now taking part in the annual Thames Sailing Barge Match, first run in 1863.

142

In 1921, as a member of the Ramsgate lifeboat crew he had taken part in the heroic rescue of the crew of the American ship "Piave", which like some of the Spanish Armada had been driven onto the notorious Goodwin Sands off Ramsgate. He had been awarded a gold medal by the President of America for his brave efforts.

The main slipway usually had on it a Thames tug for overhaul and the eastern gully provided moorings for a number of fishing boats used for laying lobster pots or taking holidaymakers for trips round Pegwell Bay. It was also home for the RNLI lifeboat and the dredger, known unkindly as the Harbour Master's yacht. Not infrequently French trawlers, seeking shelter from a coming storm, tied up alongside the west pier. Crewed by fishermen who were at sea for several days at a time, both boats and crew had a powerful smell that floated down wind before them, a mixture of fish, diesel oil and very unwashed bodies. They lived in a small cabin without sufficient headroom for me to stand up straight. Bunks on three sides and a glowing coke stove in the centre, flat topped for cooking. The heat was stifling. On several occasions I was invited to go below for a drink when I had been obliged to moor alongside while waiting for high tide and the lock gates to the inner harbour to be opened. They were very friendly, some boats had a boy of perhaps fourteen in the crew and I was given to understand he was there as a punishment for some offence. The trawler for him was a sort of open prison.

During the 1960s the London dockers sealed their own fate. A series of strikes that had become part of daily life brought the vast London docks to a standstill. Shippers resorted to using other smaller, union free ports and then increasingly containerisation. Ramsgate became one of them as did many small ports around the country. By 1980 the whole network of London docks together with the tugs, lines of long barges and acres of warehouses was dead. Dockers were largely replaced by huge containers, which can be unloaded and delivered to a customer's door with no manhandling whatsoever.

When I was born the Queen Mary, launched two years before my birth, was the largest ship afloat at 75,000 tons. Super tankers are now a quarter of a mile in length and at the time of writing "Jahre Viking", recently scrapped, over 1,500ft (458m) long was the largest ship ever built. She weighed 564,763 tons. Seven-and-a-half Queen Marys.

Nowadays Ramsgate's new breakwater outer harbour handles cross Channel ferries and large transport vessels while the inner and old outer harbour are marinas crowded with millions of pounds worth of large, comfortable yachts and motor cruisers many of which for some strange reason seldom if ever leave their moorings. Countrywide the owners of them bring much needed work and money to many British seaside resorts. Their economies collapsed with the introduction by Ramsgate man, Freddie Laker, of his no frills cheap flights and holidays abroad in 1964.

Boat building

I became interested in sailing. Martin sat next to me at school, He was the son of a tug skipper who had been killed during the war. He lived at St Peter's, Broadstairs, and had become a junior member of the newly formed Broadstairs Sailing Club. Ted Heath, later Prime Minister, was then also an active sailing member. We talked endlessly about boats and spent our uninteresting lessons, i.e. those at which we were hopeless, designing them. Here was an opportunity missed by the maths and physics

143

masters. Had our lessons involved airflow over sails, calculations of centres of effort, the relationship between the length and breadth of a dinghy to its potential speed, we would have become star pupils. Children need to see a reason for learning some things.

At twelve or thirteen I hung around the harbour whistling the tunes of old sea shanties learnt at school in the hopes that some elderly seaman would recognise a soulmate and tell me tales of his adventures. It failed to work. Not all was lost however. A three masted square rigged ship due for the scrap yard arrived to become a tourist attraction. Named the "Bounty" she had formally gloried under the name "Alistair", registered in Hango. Her rigging was intact though probably unseaworthy, but she looked the part. *(See picture p10)*. I lacked the two shillings and sixpence necessary to gain admission but sat on a bollard nearby just to hear, for the first time in my life, the strains of an electric Hawaiian guitar. I thought it absolutely magical. A year later at fifteen-and-a-half I was rich and tall enough to gain entry, although strictly not old enough to enter licensed premises. There I watched my one and only demonstration of hypnotism which formed part of the shipboard entertainment.

Noting my interest in boats my father arranged for me to go out in a Clipper class dinghy with a Broadstairs baker customer who was also a member of the club. I was hooked, joined the club and told my father I would like a boat. He laughed and mockingly said: "Then you'll need to build one". To his surprise I did and got a great deal of satisfaction overcoming the construction problems I met along the way. One of my grandfather's stores had a raised wooden floor to facilitate loading onto carts and later, lorries. Below this was a considerable collection of used timber of all sizes. Grandpa wasted nothing. He was a horder and a collector of things that he purchased at auction sales, these varied from second-hand bakery gear to stuffed birds under glass domes to swords and bayonets. I still have a Viennese bronze mouse and a bronze toad that graced his high sloping Dickensian desk as paperweights. I suspect the toad had slid down the slope and fallen on several occasions as its legs are somewhat twisted.

I begged a chunk of floor space in the store and the use of any of the timber to start my dinghy and over a period of about a year with the aid of a rusty saw put together the framework. As I recall, the task of cutting the timber to size was often too daunting with this limited equipment, so the stern thwart for instance, was about two and a half inches thick, while the framework was made from boxes that had held desiccated coconut.

Grandpa got the man who used to make the canvas covers for his horse drawn carts to sew a canvas skin over the framework for me. It was at that point I realised I had made the frame without any clear idea of how it was to be clad. He had solved the problem for me. It needed linseed oil to make it impervious to water but that cost money and I had almost none. I "borrowed" cooking oils of various sorts from his store instead, and from somewhere I begged a broken, hollow wooden mast, the remains of which I reduced to the scale of my three-and-a half metres long vessel.

It was to be a balanced gunter rig, that is to say having one sail supported on a gaff made from an ashwood baker's peel handle. The centreboard and rudder were cut from a lovely old mahogany tabletop. The mast rigging was of eighth inch galvanised fencing wire and the main halyard hoisted over a clothes line pulley wheel. I carved the name "Tadpole" on a remaining morsel of mahogany, screwed it to the transom and with my father took it to Ramsgate harbour one Saturday afternoon and launched it. To my amazement it floated in about three inches of water. At fifteen I was the youngest boat builder in the town though I have to confess it failed to bring me fame or fortune. A few weeks earlier Brian had launched his pram dinghy there and we had our first sail together without a competent helmsman. We also had our first undignified capsize within five minutes of launching during which I nearly drowned by managing to get trapped beneath the sail and swam the length of the mast instead of going sideways.

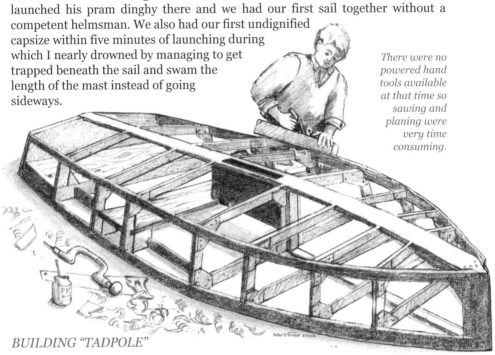

There were no powered hand tools available at that time so sawing and planing were very time consuming.

BUILDING "TADPOLE"

I thought "Tadpole" a very elegant dinghy but the harbour staff christened her the "Crab" and shouted at me every time I sailed her outside the harbour. I feigned deafness and as my competence improved the shouting stopped.

Exams and a change of course

I have included overleaf a copy of my last school report for those of you finding yourselves in a similar situation, or for your distraught parents. It fails to report my non-academic work as that is often regarded as unimportant. Academic achievement is not everything in life. School reports are usually written by teachers who have never left school. They started at five-years-old and are still there. If in doubt about anything they can always pass the buck by falling back on the headmaster for advice. They have little experience of an unprotected life in the commercial world, where you are required to make your own decisions, or that of the professional sportsman, artist, film camera man, interior designer, war corre-spondent, chef. There are plenty of ways to make your way in the world if you are an imaginative, hardworking individual. Friends who dropped out of school around the same time as me all ended up starting their own businesses and have, like me had very interesting lives. A good plumber does as well financially

KENT EDUCATION COMMITTEE

Chatham House County Grammar School, Ramsgate

REPORT on *Drake, Peter Douglas* .... Age.15 — 5.

.... *Summer* .... Term, 1951.

Form. 4. T .. of 22. boys.   Final Position... 21 .   Average Age. 15 — 3

SUBJECT	%	Position	REMARKS
English	40	=19	Disappointing. He is very unsystematic in his approach to work. *NJB*
History...	27	22	Lack of real interest or serious effort. *C.S.*
Geography	36	19	Very disappointing. His work has fallen off. *9*
French	24	15	He has tried. Can he keep his mind on anything for more than a minute? show me *W.P.P.*
German, Latin, Spanish or Biology			
Mathematics	16	22	Extremely weak. He "dreams" & is most inattentive. I see no hope for him next year. *G.S.B.*

P.T.O.

Physics or ~~General Science~~ ...	26	16	apathetic - poor results. *EPP*
Chemistry	18	17	Has neither interest or ability here. *D.P.*
Handicraft ~~and/or~~ Mechanical Drawing ...	41	19	Capable of producing really good work. Quality good, but he is too slow. *DAS PanR.*
Drawing			
Physique and Physical Education			Height... 5' 11½" ... Weight. 9st. 5lb. ... Chest. 30½ - 34"
Fortnightly Classes			3 | 3 | 3 | | |

4M N/48 57/92

House Master's Report. He has helped us with Art in the Chapman Cup. The situation as regards his work is alarming *ND*

Form Master's Report. He continues to disappoint. One can only hope that he will develop some power of concentration before long. *NJB*

Head Master's Report. He lives in a world of his own. He gives no trouble. I sometimes wish he did. *W. P. Pearce*   Head Master.

The next term will begin on... 13 SEP 1951 ...at 9 a.m. and end on... 19 DEC 1951

as a good doctor in today's world and does not normally have to turn out in the middle of the night.

It was unfortunate that the building of my dinghy had coincided with revision for my mock 'O' levels. I was fifteen and I failed. Failed disastrously. No trouble at all in art, machine drawing and woodwork, but I believe I broke all records with my 10% results in all three maths and all three science subjects and French. French was best with 13%. When the school year ended I went to work in the family business for the summer to earn money for a holiday which was spent at a Methodist youth hostel in Guernsey. I was the first member of our small family to holiday "abroad". There were still plenty of signs of the island's occupation by the Germans, concrete bunkers and gun emplacements. Barbed wire still in position in places, but it was delightful. My first holiday alone. Well not quite alone, my cousin and most of the Methodist Youth Club came as well. It was during this holiday that my grandfather had my dinghy's skin fitted. as a surprise for me.

Clearly I was not cut out to be an academic. I wanted to go to Canterbury College of Art. When school restarted my father accompanied me to a meeting with the headmaster who agreed that for once I was right. It was a good idea that I should not waste the time of his staff any further. The next day my father sneekily took me to an interview at Canterbury Technical College. I deliberately blew it. When asked by the Principal why I wanted to go there I answered that I didn't want to at all. I wanted to go to Art School. He had seen my portfolio and obligingly picked up the phone and without consulting my father asked the Principal there if he could see me, he agreed and twenty minutes later I met Mr Moody. He looked at my folder of work and I was in. No more worry about "O" or "A" level exams. That was Monday 29 October 1951. I began the following day. I loved it. To start with there were girls. I was on a general course, furniture making, silver-smithing and design for both, graphic design, drawing, painting, letterpress printing practice and theory. My father hoped silversmithing would capture my interest as he had a silversmith friend, who he believed would employ me if I was up to scratch. Again he was to be frustrated. I spent the better part of a term cutting out a circle of flat copper sheet and alternately heating it, plunging it into acid to clean it then beating it with a hammer until it resembled the shape I had drawn in the design class. One holds the metal onto a slightly domed anvil and strikes the upper surface outside the area intended for the base with the hammer which has a rounded head thereby expanding it little by little. Theoretically each blow is of identical force to maintain an even expansion all round the vessel. As the term came to towards its end the thing did start to resemble a coffee pot. The finishing touch was to braise on a thin half round collar to the outside of the rim. Heating the pot to the required cherry red I melted an irreparable hole through its side ending any hope of becoming a silversmith.

My favourite subjects were printing, drawing and painting and I would have happily done them all weekend as well, in fact often did. I lived with a sketch book and drew anything and everything, but there was a catch. To enter the printing industry one had to serve as an apprentice and had to be under seventeen at its commencement then serve for five years. Art could be followed at any age.

147

Printing

Printers were only allowed one apprentice for every six employees to ensure that there was no exploitation or unemployment. This presumably tallied with the retirement rate. My father had a school friend who was a partner in the Thanet Advertiser, a local printing works; he agreed to take me as an apprentice, known in the trade as a "printers devil". Good only to make tea, sweep the floor and melt down the metal used in the Linotype machines to cast lines of type instead of using individual letters. Also, for exciting variety, to wash up the printing machines when their minders had finished with a particular colour. Very dirty work.

Letterpress printing had changed very little from the days of William Caxton in the 1400s. Basically letters and pictures with reversed images are fixed in a frame then have ink rolled onto them, after which paper is pressed onto the inky surface. I found it all fascinating. Its ancient trade Guild and quaint terminology, its annual outing called a "Wayzgoose", and its strange spacing measurements of thins, mids, thicks, ens, ems and quads. The company was still using remnants of pre-standardisation type sizes from Victorian times with names like ruby, pearl, brevier and long primer. True the machines were powered by electricity. Ink and type were produced by others, but the typesetting and basics were still the same. Indeed we had a hundred-year-old Albion press in daily use as did several local printers. The hours were long. A basic week of 48 hours plus two evenings a week to produce a local newspaper. On news nights we had an hour to go home and get dinner then worked until the job was finished, sometimes four or five o'clock in the morning. Daily work started at 8am but following very late nights we did not have to be in until nine. If later than that we lost part of our overtime pay no matter what time we had finished the previous night. Once a week I attended Canterbury Art College to study for my City and Guilds examination.

This Albion Press was hi-tec in the 1800s and was still in daily use when I was apprenticed, both as a proofing press and to print the race cards for the local dog racing track and short runs of posters. This company was far from alone in the use of an old hand press. Another, a couple of hundred yards away was still using one designed in America, a Columbian Press, with a magnificent eagle counterweight but of similar age as was the Kent Messenger in Canterbury.

It was during my second year that I caused everyone to get extra overtime. The ancient Wharfdale Two Feeder news machine had to be hand fed with individual sheets of paper large enough to take four broadsheet pages on each side,

This was my indenture for five years of my life. I doubt if many young people of today would be very content with either the pay or the terms of the contract, however it served me well as at the end of it I had a good understanding of the technology and was able to open my own business a couple of years after the apprenticeship finished.

This Apprenticeship Deed made the 21st day of July 195 2

BETWEEN Peter Douglas Drake of 66, Park Road,
Ramsgate in the County of Kent (hereinafter called
"the Apprentice") Son of Douglas Walter Drake of the same place of the
first part, the said Douglas Walter Drake (hereinafter called "the Parent")
of the second part, and Thanet Advertiser Ltd.
of Church Hill, Ramsgate, in the County of
. Kent (hereinafter called "the Employer")
of the third part: **Witnesseth** and it is hereby agreed as follows:—

1. The Apprentice of his own free will with the consent and approbation of the Parent (testified by his execution of this deed) puts and binds himself Apprentice to the Employer to learn the Art, Trade or Business of a Printer

and with him after the manner of an Apprentice to serve for the term of five years from the at day of July 1952 .

2. **During** the said term the Apprentice shall :—

(1) Faithfully serve the Employer, his secrets keep, and his lawful commands obey ;

(2) Do no damage to the Employer or to his goods, nor suffer such damage to be done by others, and forthwith give notice to the Employer of the same when necessary ;

(3) Not waste the goods of the Employer nor lend them unlawfully to any person, nor do any act whereby the Employer may sustain any loss ;

(4) Not without the consent of the Employer buy nor sell on his behalf, nor absent himself from the Employer's service without leave ;

(5) In all things behave himself as a faithful Apprentice towards the Employer and others having authority over him.

3. In considerat (the receipt of which sum during the said term as instructed the Apprentice or relating thereto.

4. The Employ

First Y	
Second	
Third Y	
Fourth Y	
Fifth Y	

4. **The Employer shall pay the Apprentice the following wages during the said term :—**

First Year	30% of Standard Rate
Second Year	35% of Standard Rate
Third Year	40% of Standard Rate
Fourth Year	50% of Standard Rate
Fifth Year	60% of Standard Rate

5. The Employ holidays or any other ho shall not be entitled to an his own default and in t the said wages a part pro

5. **The** Employer shall not be entitled to make any deduction from the said wages in respect of the usual holidays or any other holiday from time to time allowed by the Employer to the Apprentice but the Apprentice shall not be entitled to any wages if and while he is absent from work through illness or other incapacity or through his own default and in the case of absence from any such cause the Employer shall be entitled to deduct from the said wages a part proportionate to the number of working hours lost through such absence.

6. If the Appr persist in absenting himself from the service of the Employer during working hours without just cause or shall otherwise misconduct himself then and in any such cases the Employer may by notice in writing determine the Apprenticeship and dismiss the Apprentice from the Employer's service.

7. This Deed shall if the provisions thereof are duly complied with by the Apprentice be delivered to the Apprentice on the completion of the said term of Apprenticeship with a Certificate of such service endorsed thereon.

8. For the true performance of all and every of the said covenants and agreements the Apprentice and the Parent on the one hand and the Employer on the other hand hereby respectively bind themselves.

In Witness whereof the parties hereto have hereunto set their hands and seals the day and year first above written.

Signed Sealed and Delivered by the parties hereto in the presence of

Hilda Solly.

a size called quad crown. The type lay on a flat bed and passed under ink rollers then beneath the printing cylinder that grips an individual sheet of paper fed in by the minder pressing it firmly to the face of the type. At the end of its revolution it returned carrying a sheet fed in by the minder on the opposite side of the cylinder. When sufficient had been printed at a speed of about 1,500 an hour the paper was turned over and another four pages printed on the reverse side. This was all repeated a second time to make a sixteen page paper, the sheets being then passed through a folding machine by two other men to combine them. Each newspaper was therefore handled six times.

One evening, instead of being the number two minder I was to be at the controls for the first time. Let me explain. At that time the machinery we used was powered by "direct current", DC, which required much larger motors than their present AC equivalents: motors whose speed had to be built up gradually by slowly feeding in the power through a box called a rheostat. The foreman forgot to tell me this last important point. When he said "Start the machine I whacked the rheostat lever from stop to start in one swift movement. There was an almighty explosion and the entire electrical panel for the building blew off the wall. Blew to bits. Large porcelain fuse carriers turned to powder. No lights, and no power. It was 7pm on a winter evening and the paper must be produced. The electricians were tracked down in their homes to put in a temporary supply, so that by 2am we were able to restart production. As everyone was paid double time after the first five hours of overtime I was quite popular with all but the foreman.

There had been a restriction of eight pages on newspapers following the war because of the lack of raw materials, so sixteen pages then seemed quite substantial. As the size of papers increased the business joined forces with the East Kent Times, just across the road with their faster, much more up-to-date Cossor press, a roll fed machine. The old Wharfdale was sold to a newspaper in Australia. Perhaps it is still going. Victorian machinery did not really wear out, it was just surpassed by later technology.

Wages for apprenticeships were appalling, but in general the outcome was a properly trained man. In my grandfather's time one had to pay to be an apprentice, in his case £30, equivalent to thirty weeks basic wages. He served his time in the grocery trade sleeping below the counter at night, but received his food and his washing was done for him. For the third year he received two shillings and sixpence a week. I was luckier. I didn't sleep under the counter or live in. My first year I was paid one pound seven shillings and six pence for a forty-eight hour week (£1.35p) Thirty percent of a tradesman's wages with gentle rises annually until in the fifth year I got sixty percent of a man's pay which had by then risen to £8.50p Now many young people starting their first job expect at least three times my first year's income each week. People were paid in cash, weekly. Few had bank accounts.

The whole method of printing has changed from letterpress to offset lithography and computers. No need for compositors to set lines of type, the journalist does it direct from his computer complete with his mistakes which are frequent, even in the Times. The pages are produced on the computer and printing plates by photography. Sunday papers are the thickness of several novels, printed in colour from a reel like a giant toilet roll, cut, folded, counted and banded ready for delivery, the machine operated by one man at speeds of 20,000 an hour or more. Letterpress printing has practically disappeared. Strange to think that all its considerable skills, honed over six centuries, have almost vanished in less than a lifetime. A few years ago I had reason to visit a printing works which had a long machine in a glass compartment operated by one man. A ton roll of paper being fed in at one end and fully bound, several hundred page holiday catalogues pouring out of the other, pre-tied in bundles ready for despatch. Amazing.

The Germans introduced this platen printing press into Britain in the late 1950s allowing 10% discount on the printer's old machine's scrap value. It had a maximum speed of 5,000 copies an hour. My foot powered treadle machine (see icon above) made 1,500 if I did well. I bought a Heidleberg in 1960 by getting a discount against a friend's scrap diesel engine as I had no spare old machine to trade in.

150

My spare time

While still at art school I had started building a Cadet pram dinghy with a waterproof Masonite hardboard skin for cheapness, this time using one of my grandfather's lockup garages as a workshop. Small boats of that era were still built of wood, mostly clinker built, overlapping planks like the Viking ships. Then increasingly from moulded ply developed during the war by Fairey Marine, or hard chine boats using sheet marine ply. Ply had the benefit of producing a much lighter craft. Now they are mostly fibreglass, moulded like jellies, while many small dinghies are entirely plastic. Building the Cadet took all my spare time for about eighteen months largely because I had insufficient money for the brass screws which I supplemented by using screws intended to hold in place the woodwork in the Southern Railway carriages that carried me to Art School each week. You are quite right, it was vandalism and inexcusable.

It was almost finished in June 1953, just needing painting. Disaster struck. A cigarette dropped in a laundry van in the main part of the garage started a fire that destroyed the entire building. The heat from it was so intense it melted the main power cable for the area buried below the adjacent public footpath and the glass from its windows ran down the street. The fire brigade, unable to save the building, used their resources to hose down our petrol pumps and the

Brian crewing for me in "Sally" in the 1954 Kent Week regatta at Ramsgate. Unable to afford oilskins we sailed in our normal clothes as did many others in those unsophisticated days. We came third that day.

fronts of houses on the opposite side of the road. That was the end of the boat. Fortunately my father gave me some of the insurance money to buy "Sally", an old clinker built Kent class dinghy which became my pride and joy for the next few years.

151

ESSEX ONE DESIGNS *The end of a race outside Ramsgate harbour before the construction of the new ferry port. The race officer on the west pierhead was a great character and friend, Surgeon Lt. Commander Sinclair Leutit, RN Rtd. owner of a vicious but muzzled bull terrier, killer of more than one peace loving alsation and his housekeeper's cat with whom it had long cohabited. Unmarried, he was the original Edwardian. When going out to dinner in a restaurant or the Club, he inspected the kitchens in the morning leaving precise instructions for opening of his wine and its temperature.*

In 1952 the town's Royal Temple Yacht Club was in a bad way. Pre-war its membership had been almost exclusively professional or substantial land owners. Many were now dead and the remainder mostly social members. About six were enthusiastic dinghy sailors and a couple of others had cruisers. Although the war had largely destroyed class distinctions I think they were unable to persuade themselves to invite the hoypaloi to join but did agree to open the club to younger members at very reduced fees. At sixteen Brian and I joined and were able to sail as crew in 18' Essex One Design races each Saturday and after a time to use them by ourselves during the week. Later as the owners aged, they still maintained the boats and had them put in the water for our use at very considerable expense to themselves. It was an extremely generous gesture. I particularly appreciated it when I had a hollow wooden mast split while beating to windward during a hard race. I apologised for the damage to Mr Hatton, the dentist owner and he said: "Don't be silly. Race to win, that's why we have insurance." Hollow wooden masts preceeded alloy, which became popular in the 60s for racing boats.

Entertainment and Socialising

Of course there were other activities in the town. Friends belonged to rugby, football, tennis and bowls clubs. In the late 60s, with the decline in cinema attendance due to television some of these buildings became bowling alleys or bingo halls. At the time there were no health clubs or gymnasiums, nor was there much need for them as the population walked a lot and fast, fatty foods had yet to wreck the nation's health.

In the days before television cinemas enjoyed great popularity. Ramsgate had four cinemas and the queues for entry were often long. In the High Street facing towards Hardres Street was the Victorian Palace Theatre, still a theatre when the war finished, it had a very large stage and an entry at the back, so that it could put on spectacular shows with horses etc. on stage. It was later converted to a cinema with a Wurlitzer organ that rose through the floor and was played during the intervals. Almost opposite, in the High Street was the Picture House. The Kings Theatre commonly called the Flea Pit nestled in a passageway off the Market Place. The Odeon in King Street was the largest and newest and also had Saturday morning films for children at six pence each. Entry normally cost between 1s:6d and 2s:6d. (Seven-and-a-half to twelve-and-a-half new pence.) There was further entertainment available on the seafront with summer variety shows and pantomimes in the Pavilion Theatre, West Cliff Hall and the newly constructed Granville Theatre, which also hosted repertory companies and Ice Shows.

There was also private entertainment, another leftover from a previous era. At family gatherings it was not uncommon, as the afternoon or evening wore on, for people to tell stories, play music, sing a song, or recite poetry. A chance to show off the gifts of one's children, frequently to the total embarrassment of the child. On free evenings at home we had jam sessions, my father on the piano, I on the 'cello, Michael on the trombone and David, still very young on the drum. Probably a horrible noise but we enjoyed it. Conversation has sadly died with the introduction of television.

The town had more than its fair share of public houses to cope with the holiday folk and locals alike. After the war the inovation of several Italian owned milk bars proved very popular. Brightly lit, selling icecream, sodas and having a jukebox, they provided meeting places for the young and courting couples as well as coffee and tea for shoppers.

Discos were non existent. After all a record then only lasted about four minutes. However there was a dance hall on the seafront below the East Cliff latterly frequented by the American airmen based at Manston. Church halls sometimes held dances for their youth clubs as did the Working Men's Club for its members. This was the time of the big bands of national fame like Jo Loss and Ted Heath or the traditional jazz of Chris Barber, Kenny Ball, Acker Bilk and the Temperance Seven. Big time bands; they played at more formal dances, usually held at Margate's Winter Gardens.

When I first started courting there were well attended dancing classes held in the ballroom of the San Clu Hotel, where we learnt to do the waltz, quickstep, foxtrot and palais glide under the eye of Florrie Hamilton. I can still hear her strident voice, "Slow, slow, quick quick, slow". My efforts have been likened by various trampled partners to those of a dancing camel. One can't be good at everything.

I do not remember my parents inviting friends to dinner parties nor being invited out to others. They were sociable folk with a wide circle of friends and visiting Church Ministers were normally invited for Sunday lunch after the morning service. I suppose it was the rationing that curtailed such entertaining, I was eighteen by the time it finished. I married at twenty-one. After that I was living away from home, only returning to my parents for frequent, large, family gatherings. I think family togetherness was more important to people then.

My friend Brian married about the same time and I recall that in the early 60s we had a regular rendezvous at his house once a week to watch the very popular comedy programme, "Hancock's Half Hour", because he had a small television. Sometimes to eat as well. There was comparatively little money about and eating out took a substantial bite out of our incomes. Apart from fish and chips there were no cheap takeaway food shops and regular restaurant meals were often beyond our means. Luckily things improved considerably over the succeeding ten years.

Games and sport

Without doubt football was the main sport, closely followed by cricket. When I passed my Eleven Plus my grandfather rewarded me by taking me to watch the local Derby of the year, Ramsgate *v* Margate. He was a keen sportsman and shared a box at the Ramsgate ground with two other local businessmen. A Past President of Thanet Wanderers Rugby Club, he was also still a keen bowls player. It was very kind of him to include me in with his friends but I had no interest in football. In the sixty years between then and now I have successfully avoided any repetition of the experience. A cricket match between Kent and Yorkshire at the Canterbury cricket ground with my father and some school friends had the same effect, but at least these games were played by local men playing for their own town or county. Just like the shin kicking matches in the north of England. For many years I had a battered, cauliflower-eared and broken-nosed friend who, prewar, had been a professional rugby player for his town. He told me that his instruction, if injured, was to ensure that he took one of the opposing side off with him.

To get me more interested in sport generally my father took me to Dover to see the torch for the first, post war Olympic games, pass through the town having just landed from France and was now enroute direct to London. I am afraid it failed to inspire me.

After every news broadcast today we have "Sport". For the most part this is a totally misleading title. This is business. Big, big business. Ramsgate could win the World Cup. All it needs is few hundred million pounds to go out and buy the best players in the world. If nationality is a problem the stranger will be quickly granted naturalisation to overcome that deficiency. Sport for me is where it is man's skill against nature that decides the outcome. Nature does not cheat, but has no mercy and the players get no great reward except the knowledge that they have overcome it. Skiing, horse racing, gliding, mountain climbing or sailing are true sports in my book. The others are just games for big money. For instance the America's Cup boats cost currently seven or eight million pounds plus months of training which earn the winners the honour of holding, for a few years, a cup that probably cost less than one of the boat's high tech winches.

154

Television

Television was invented before the war and the BBC transmitted for about four hours a day between 1936 and September 1939 when it was put on hold for the war years, restarting in June 1946. In the years immediately after hostilities ceased it took a while to rebuild factories and change production lines for peaceful products. This was considerably hampered by a terrible lack of materials of all sorts. Entertainment was not top of the recovery list nor did the population have the money to lavish on luxuries.

As I recall, the expansion took off with the desire of everyone to see the Coronation of Queen Elizabeth II in 1952. That was my first look at the new wonder at the house of a friend. The picture on those early television sets was not at all the quality of those of today. Large H shaped aerials sprouted on chimneys and small ones sat on, or near, the set. These last had to be very carefully adjusted to capture the black and white picture which often appeared to be viewed through a violent snow storm. The screens in 1953 were quite small by present day standards at 15" (28cm) and the tubes frequently died after a year or two of use. They were very expensive to replace. The following year 17" (42cm) seems to have become the basic size and prices had dropped from an average of £80 to £70, a sum equivalent to about eight weeks wages. We had our first in 1954.

It was sets like this 1952 Bush that introduced television to the British public who were able to watch a coronation for the first time, that of Queen Elizabeth II. Also, a few years later, the start of the serial Coronation Street.

The set was full of glass valves, similar to light bulbs. Transistors and solid state electronics were first introduced into radios in 1955 and televisions in 1958. Rediffusion was a company that had previously provided good quality sound to subscribers by wire. It now moved into the television field renting out TV receivers without many of the components, but again using their superior aerial to capture and redistribute the picture by wire to their clientele.

BBC transmissions in colour did not commence until 1966 and the ones I first saw were a rather pasty colour, but rapidly improved. For a number of years the new medium suffocated the film industry. Many cinemas all over the country were converted into bingo halls and bowling alleys or supermarkets before returning to become multiscreen cinemas towards the end of the century. Family conversation has largely died out as a result of television. Meals formerly eaten around the dinner table, where the day's events could be discussed have given way to many taking their meals on their lap in front of the new god. Their conversations perhaps transferred to their mobiles.

Icecream, love and politics

At seventeen the two summer loves of my life were sailing and icecream. Girlfriends were for the winter months, however that year priorities changed slightly. After a race I treated myself to an icecream and stopped at a harbourside stall. At that moment there were no other customers and I stayed to chat to the student whose summer job was selling the new fashion Softerfreeze ices. I learned that she was starting work as a junior reporter on the same newspaper as myself at the end of the season. She gave me a large icecream for nothing and became my regular port of call for more icecream at the end of each Saturday afternoon race.

In due course she started work and became my girlfriend and some years later my wife. We had one problem, she had often to work in the evening covering local events and meetings so we went together. There were political meetings leading up to local elections, where the father of a work colleague was hoping to stand as the Communist candidate. He was a council worker well known to me and was in charge of three men, I never saw more. I think their job was small repairs like repainting lampposts or replacing broken paving. In those pre-car days a six foot long hand barrow was the normal way of transporting ladders, tools and small amounts of material. His job was apparently to walk beside them. He was above a barrow pusher so had spare breath to expound on the leaches of society who were in cushy jobs like working in shops or offices, or worse still, capitalist owners of such establishments. All very laudable stuff but I could not help noticing when they came to a hill, and they are not rare in Ramsgate, he did not lower himself to the level of a pusher. Perhaps by then he had run out of breath.

The Communist Party meeting was held in the local Workingmen's Club where, after an introductory address to the comrades, a visiting speaker gave a somewhat lengthy speech then the meeting was thrown open to the floor. Speaker number one leapt to his feet and expounded for about twenty minutes, I forget the subject but, like myself, the chairman felt it time to move on and rapped his gavel for silence. Number one continued unabated. After a few minutes the chairman tried again, but the speaker was completely unstoppable. Again the gavel hammered the table to no effect so the chairman indicated to speaker number two, on the opposite side of the room, that he should commence. He did, at full throttle and we were treated to stereoscopic sound. Neither side gave an inch and the chaos continued for about five minutes after which the faithful started to drift towards the bar or the door. We left with them.

The Liberals were often Chapel folk, kindly, decent, honest people who just wanted the best for everybody but seemed to have no particular overall policy or priority and lacked any spirited leadership. The Labour Party certainly had the spirited leaders and considerable funds as most industrial workers of the period were obliged to belong to a union to get a job, myself included, and were expected to pay a levy on their wages towards the Party funds. Their claims were for increased wages or better conditions for the workers rather than for the general good. The elderly, sick and unemployed had no champion. I backed the Conservatives whose meetings were run in an orderly manner by men who were mostly employers or businessmen on the basis that they apparently understood how to organise things properly. If the grass roots of an organisation rose to the management of it, for me this party seemed the best chance of doing a proper job.

156

Transport

Cars were mostly old, a luxury enjoyed by very few. When I started my apprentice-ship in 1952, of the twenty-two staff only the two directors had cars. The editor had a sports car and the Works Director, the small Ford 8 saloon, both of pre-war vintage. Three men had motorbikes, two of them with sidecars to accommodate their family. Vespa scooters started to appear in 1952. The rest of us fell back on Grandma's Shanks pony or had push bikes. I believe this represented a fairly normal cross section of the population. Come to think of it, we never had need to lock our bikes and I cannot remember ever hearing of one being stolen. Certainly in the provinces people were much less light fingered than now.

Driving licence renewable every 3 years, no photo required.

Victorian Bath chairs were still for sale in 1936.

When I was 23 I launched myself into the business world in the smallest way possible by buying from a retired man for £120 his run down printing enter-prise which had an average weekly gross turnover of £5. Much of his time had been spent socialising in a local club. Like almost all my contemporaries, I had no transport other than a push bike. As the business was carried out in a small shed in Birchington, some five miles away, I was obliged to obtain a second-hand Cyclemaster, a bike with a motor set in the rear wheel. A year or so later I paid £6.50 for a 1937 Austin 7 Ruby saloon. *(See icon)* With the help of a friend I rebuilt the engine and resold the car at a modest profit then bought for £10 a 1939 Lanchester pictured on the previous page. It was a lovely piece of machinery with leather seats, an aluminium body and super engine and Daimler gearbox. Unfortunately one day the rear nearside wheel overtook me on the offside as I was slowing down near a junction. The half shaft had broken. Again I became a mechanic after searching the breakers yards. That was the last time in my life as I have no gift for machinery, too many damaged knuckles when the spanner slips. All cars of the period carried a starting handle which could be inserted through the front below the radiator into the end of the crankshaft for manual starting if the battery failed.

These car manufacturing companies and many more, like Rolls Royce, Rover, Standard, Vauxhall, Morgan, Humber and MG were British, but gradually swallowed up in mergers, sold to foreign competitors or destroyed by union conflicts. Thousands of jobs gone in the wind just like shipbuilding. We changed from being a major producer into a stockist for foreign producers. Endless union. strikes for more pay and apathy regarding quality control handed it all to the Far East and our European competitors.

Local public transport was mostly on East Kent's red double-decker buses with a service every five minutes on principle routes between Ramsgate and Margate. From Southampton to the Medway towns and mid Kent was the preserve of the green buses of the Southdown Bus Company founded by my great grandfather's brother-in-law. When his maiden daughter died many years later she left her fortune to the RSPCA, but not a penny to the woman who had cared for her.

Southern Railway steam trains were available for longer journeys. For the rapid transport of goods the service was better than rail can provide at the present time. My grandfather could order yeast from Holland one day and expect it to arrive in Harwich on the overnight ferry; it would be transferred to the railway and arrive in Ramsgate that afternoon. Similarly eggs ordered in Normandy by telegram would arrive two days later. The railways were nationalised on the 1st January 1948 to form British Railways. Their Red Star service enabled goods to travel on the rail network for guaranteed same day delivery. A service no longer available, the business is now handled by international goods distributors who undertake world wide deliveries by road and air. It is a shame that instead of improving the rail system as has happened in France and other countries, the Labour Government saw fit to massively reduce the rail network causing far more traffic onto the already overcrowded roads. They then destroyed many of the bridges and missed a great opportunity in many regions to create bridle paths, or footpaths, along land isolated from motor traffic which, after all, having been nationalised, belonged to the nation and could have provided a wonderful nationwide safe passage for activities such as walking, riding and cycleways, reducing the hazards of the road.

In the 40s and 50s deliveries were by barrow, trades bike, van or lorry and in the case of the local pubs sometimes by steam driven Foden lorries, rarely in the 50s by horse and cart. Lorries and vans were of much more modest size than those of today with a maximun vehicle weight of 17 tons increased in 1983 to 38 tons and in 2003 to 44 tons. In the 1930s most vans were simply replacements for their horse drawn predecessors. A horse pulled 30cwt. (One and a half tons.) There were still a number of horse drawn vehicles in the town on which to hitch a ride to the annoyance of the carters. Pulling a milk float the horse got to know the round as well as its driver, pausing while he made a delivery and moving on to the next house as soon as it heard the empties dropped back into a crate. Bill Matthews our coalman, a greengrocer of forgotten name and also the rag and bone men continued with horses as before; and as before we kids hung on the back if we got the chance.

A 30 cwt Bedford van was less intelligent and more expensive than a horse, but was faster and did not need feeding or mucking out.

Deafness

A little "By the way":-

Battery operated hearing aids were not yet on the scene in 1936. Life was very difficult for the hard of hearing. With the arrival of transistors in the mid fifties things became easier for those with hearing loss. Aids have been miniaturised to the point where they are almost invisible and now cochlea implants hide the problem completely. The little gem on the right was available for those who suffered hearing loss, however I would suppose that if the speaker was that close to the person's ear it would hardly be necessary.

Transport of babies has made great changes since I occupied a pram. Gone are the great Silver Cross prams of yesteryear, rightly described as baby carriages, completely blocking the hallway. Now you can almost get one in an umbrella stand. Invalid carriages of my youth are forgotten as people of my age hurtle down the street in electrically powered chairs. In the 30s it was still possible to buy a Victorian wicker Bath chair *(p157)* and be pushed along the seafront while issuing instructions to one's chauffeur listening to his responses with an ear trumpet. Later invalid carriages had a chain drive where the person wound a pair of handles like bike pedals to propel himself.

Ear Trumpet, each 16/-

Road Safety

My father started driving in the mid 1920s at which time there were no driving licences. When I started in 1953 the test was simple; drive, emergency stop, reverse into a side road and park neatly, two or three questions on road signs and away you went. Highway Codes were much thinner documents, the profusion of signs far less. In 1960 a test for vehicles over ten years old was introduced, the MOT annual Road Test certificate in 1967. Until then we often drove until the canvas showed on our tyres. Pre-1960 cars lacked many of the conveniences we now expect in them. Windscreens were flat, subject to glare; no screen washing equipment, so that mud sprayed up by the car in front was smeared by the single wiper across one's vision. The driver was frequently obliged to work it manually with a small lever on the motor inside, just above the windscreen in front of him, when the dirt friction was too great for it. Rod brakes would stop the car if properly adjusted and were given sufficient time, but there was no test require-ment to check them. No brake lights, drivers wound down their window and waved their arm up and down to indicate their intention to slow down, or with a rotary motion to turn left and straight out for a right turn. Cars had no heating so travelling rugs were very necessary. Indicators were fitted in the centre door pillar each side at about the height of the driver's head; turn the indicator switch and an orange indicator, lit from within and about 5 x 20 cm swivelled out to the horizon-tal, if they did not, one gave the door pillar a clout and out they popped. On the plus side, they had no radio and the drivers were not distracted by mobile phones. Cars were generally made of thicker material and had proper bumpers.

There were much greater numbers of motorcycles on the road in the 40s and 50s and the choice was vast, names like Velocette, Bown, Brough, BSA, Matchless, Ariel, Douglas, Scott, Sunbeam and dozens more. Families had a motorbike with a sidecar attached. With two on the bike and two small children in the sidecar travel was comparatively cheap. Motorcyclists seldom wore crash helmets, if they did the helmets looked like half a football with a chin strap. For most of us it was bikes or walk.

The Automobile Association

In my childhood and for many years to come the country was sprinkled with AA boxes, like this one, on all major roads. Those that remain are now listed buildings though not in use. Mobile phones were almost half-a-century in the future so the AA issued keys for these boxes to all members. With it one could gain entry to any box and use its phone to call their reception centre and obtain help. Assistance arrived in the form of a bright yellow motorbike with a sidecar containing their mechanic's equipment. The rider wore buff coloured jodphurs and riding boots, their uniform always reminded me of the Canadian Mounted Police. In addition to their key, members were given a 3" high badge to mount on their radiator or bumper so that the patrolman would easily recognise them. As one drove past the patrolman would salute. Very quaint you may think, but there was more than politeness to it. If he failed to salute customers would stop to enquire why. The AA man could then advise them of a speed trap, accident or deviation to the route.

Stress

Today great attention is paid to people subject to stress, particularly those who have experienced great horrors, for instance those involved in the 9/11 attack in America. During the great world wars men who broke down under the strain were often shot or imprisoned for acts seen as cowardice. When the last war ended more and more people realised that some of the returning troops had been subjected to unimaginable horrors, not once, not for a week, but for years on end. A man I saw regularly on the way to and from school, arriving at the curb to cross the road he would snap to attention, face back the way he had come, salute, turn round again and march across the road. Where he was in his imagination I have no idea but it was very sad to see a comparatively young man in this state. now that we were once again at peace.

I gained a small insight into the sort of unrelenting stress soldiers could experience a few years later in conversations with a work colleague, Harry Handy. Harry had fought in the Far East against the Japanese for four years. He told me about nightly guard duty in the inky blackness of the jungle, vegetation so thick that even in daylight if one stretched out a hand it disappeared in the greenery. Often through his lonely watch he could hear movements, rustlings, creakings and Japanese with speaking trumpets saying "Hello Tommy", "We can see you Tommy", "We are coming to get you Tommy". Waiting all the time for the duty to end or a knife to slide silently into his back. He found this much harder to put up with than actual action. Whether Donkey *(page 140)* had experienced this sort of thing I do not know.

Harry was also a source of wisdom and a good friend. There was a period when I was very short of money and newly married and far too proud to ask my father for help, so I talked to him about my worries. He said: "When I docked in China there were bodies floating around the ship each day. As we marched we passed bodies of starved families lying in the streets. In convoys across the mountains the road would suddenly give way and a lorry would slide over the edge of a precipice taking whole families with it. The Chinese would look down the cliff face, shrug, and start digging further into the hillside to reinstate the road. How many dead or starving people have you seen lying around here. Don't worry. In England everyone survives." At times, when I have had what seemed to me serious trouble, his words have come back to cheer me.

Clothes

The amount of clothing commonly worn by people in the first half of the 1900s would stifle those of today. Cotton, wool, linen and silk were the available materials. Money was tight so things were made to last. If you could return to those days I think the most noticeable difference would be the comparative drabness except for the really wealthy. You would find no jeans, tee shirts, trainers, or designer clothes and certainly none bearing the name of the manufacturer on the outside. Hats on many boys and girls and most adults. Businessmen and male office staff, or shop salesmen, wore a vest, shirt and tie under a suit with a waistcoat. Many carried umbrellas because they were on foot. . . . and in Britain.

Babies were born and wrapped in a cotton sheet carefully imprisoning their arms by their sides, rigid, like little Egyptian mummies, in the belief it was necessary to ensure their bones grew straight. No disposable, leakproof, fling-it-in-the-bin gear. White towelling nappies, sometimes over a soft muslin one. Afterwards rinse, wash and dry ready for next time. As I recall one bought 24 nappies for a child. During the war these later became dusters or face clothes when the baby no longer needed them.

To protect baby from the cold and make sure its bones kept straight it wore a vest and over it a liberty bodice, like a waistcoat with taped seams and edges and soft cotton material buttons down the front. The tape helped to stiffen it. The liberty bodice was discarded well before school age. Boys universally wore shorts until they were thirteen and girls a dress or blouse and skirt and a cardigan. Never trousers.

162

I have included these boring family groups to illustrate the subtle changes brought about by rationing. The first was taken just after the outbreak of war and the second in 1949. You will notice that the fabric of the womens' dresses above is pleated and full cut. The restrictions of war not yet started to bite. Below, the dresses are shorter and more substantial, made to last, stiffer, with the exception of a couple of the older women who have retained their pre-war dresses. The boys in shorts, clearly not yet thirteen.
The haircuts are standard for the era, no shaven heads or punk cuts. As I recall, the dramatic changes in hair fashion started with Elvis Presley who was copied by Teddy Boy gangs (see icon) in the mid 1950s.

At school age we boys generally wore a white cotton vest under a grey shirt during the autumn and winter. Made with a high percentage of wool for additional warmth these shirts were itchy companions when new. Over this a sleeveless V-neck wool pullover and a grey jacket of wool worsted with matching shorts. In wet weather this was all covered with a navy blue knee length macintosh woven so tightly it was fairly waterproof for short periods. Spring and summer shirts were white above light brown corduroy shorts which after repeated washing ended up nearer cream, except for tar stains collected playing marbles in the road. Girls had a blouse and gymslip, (a sort of pleated skirt with a bib front) and white socks. Boys wore long grey socks with the tops folded over elastic garters to hold them up. There were of course variations of blazer colour when reaching secondary school if it had a uniform. Mine often smelt rather off as I used to transport a white mouse with me. It slept in my pocket most of the day, but as a breeder of mice, not a difficult skill, I did quite a reasonable business with other boys who wanted to own one. I do remember wearing wellington boots made the backs of our legs very sore.

Before the war city folk with the inclination to lead fashion could be far from drab. This aunt was the furs buyer for an Oxford Street store and must have caused quite a stir in this red and white outfit in 1939.

Women had considerable underpinnings. A vest and a corset with flattened springs in it to give support and squash the wearer to her desired shape, a suspender belt to hold up her stockings, a bra and one or more petticoats to hold out her dress. From the clothing point of view women suffered the most during the war. The fine cottons and silks became unobtainable during the rationing. Sturdiness and longevity outweighed delicacy and fashion. Wartime styles had to use the minimum necessary for decency and decency at that time was ten centimetres below the knee. For the first time ever in the UK women could be found in trousers, working in factories or on the land. When the war finished I recall one local draper, Lewis & Hyland, acquired a load of silk parachutes which sold like hot cakes to ladies with dressmaking skills.

Post-war trade with cotton producing countries saw dresses becoming fuller and longer. Pleated and dirndal skirts full enough to fly out flat when the wearer spun round fast dancing to jive and rock. (See the best known picture of Marilyn Monroe.) This was a period when fashion changed each year, I suppose to make up for the years of austerity. It came to an end with Mary Quant's mini in 1966 after which anything went. Long, full flowing Indian type dresses, minis so short they exposed everthing unless the wearer remained absolutely vertical, trouser suits, jeans, whatever suited the wearer's mood.

Menswear in the thirties, forties and fifties changed surprisingly little. Shirts from the forties onwards were mostly collar attached, whereas many older men stuck to hard starched, detachable collars frequently rounded rather than pointed at the corners. Suits usually had a waistcoat. Labourers often used a collarless shirt and an old waistcoat, office workers were expected to turn up to work wearing a suit and tie. Men of my grandfather's age might change to a light alpaca jacket over their waistcoat in the summer, but otherwise wore the same clothes they used in winter, i.e. vest, shirt and tie, waistcoat and suit. Perhaps more casual at weekends with slacks, and sports jacket or pullover. The cap or trilby hat exchanged for a straw boater or panama hat. Hats enjoyed far more popularity with men, women and children than at present. *(See the picture of Molly p47.)* City men wore "Cokes", known more familiarly as bowlers.

About 1956 Teddy Boys, gangs of youths out looking for trouble, developed a style of their own. Hair in the exaggerated Elvis Presley fashion, high quiff at the front and ducks tail behind. The whole supported with a generous helping of Brylcream. They wore black drape jackets, longer than normal with black velvet collars and paid a fortune for them. Their black trousers, called drainpipes because of their very narrow cut, set off the extra thick crepe soled shoes and gave the whole ensemble a top heavy look. Dressed like that one gang would go out looking for another to fight, Ramsgate versus Margate or Southend, as long as there was a good scrap. A few fellows stabbed, bottles broken over heads. Completely stupid but at least confined to themselves.

For one year during the war my father made me wear boots. Heavy black workman's style. I detested them as I was the only one in the class who had them. After that it was plain black shoes, all leather of course, except that shoes were frequently resoled with rubber. Steel studs called Blakeys, the name of their manufacturer, were hammered in around the heels and toes to help resist wear. Many families had a shoe last, a sort of iron foot, on which to effect their own repairs. We had one, shoes had to last, clothing coupons were so valuable. Fast growing children's feet required footwear to be passed down to younger brothers and sisters. In summer we wore brown crepe soled sandals.

Life has changed dramatically. The introduction of nylon after the end of the war, then other synthetic fabrics, has revolutionised clothing and bedding. Drip dry materials save hours of ironing. We have clothes at remarkable prices from the Far East. Central heating and duvets have rendered bedmaking almost a thing of the past, just snap on an undersheet and a fresh duvet cover. It's done. Before, there was a bottom sheet to tuck in all round followed by a top sheet and several blankets again needing to be tucked in under the heavy mattress, on top of that lot an eiderdown and bedspread and a hot water bottle during the cold months. Bedrooms seldom had heating unless the occupant was ill. Washing machines and dryers now take automatic care of three days of a woman's working week while she is at the office, watching HD television, or out with her family.

Personal adornment in the form of tattoos has come into fashion. In my youth it was almost entirely the province of gypsies and sailors or Forces men who had been stationed abroad and drunk rather too much one night. Jewellery for men was confined to a signet ring. Today we see incredible amounts of ironmongery attached to the most unlikely parts of peoples bodies. Our grandparents would be amazed and horrified by it. Perhaps the next generation of grandchildren will feel the same, viewing the by then, wrinkled bodies of this one. "Dad, does Grandad wear woad because he's an ancient Briton?"

Recordings and sound amplification

Music was a passion of my father although his record collection was meagre to say the least, about a dozen shellac discs 12"dia (30cms) playable on both sides, well worn because the hand wound gramophone used steel or hard fibre needles to pick up the sound. *(See icon)* If it was a long record, and by long I mean over three minutes, it was necessary to start winding again as the sound slowly became lower and lower down the scale and more and morre drawwnn oowwwt. At Lamberhurst this had been our only entertainment other than the radio. While there we had a couple of favourites, "I fell for a lady from Oopsalah" and "Mares eat oats and does eat oats but little lambs eat ivy, diddly divey doe". All great for little children. Then something for mixed ages, two pieces by Katelbey, "In a Monastery Garden" and "In a Persian Market". (I have since been in both, in my case the market resulted in a painting instead of music). The rest were Beethoven, Mozart and choral, and part of the Messiah. For the most part he preferred to play, or sing, the music himself to enjoy the true sound. He and the generations before him only heard really great, accurate sound at concerts like the Proms at London's Albert Hall, similar concert halls or great cathedrals. Those of meagre income perhaps just a few times in their lives. Perhaps never. Now we can hear it without giving it a second thought.

Battery operated portable record players appeared in the early 1950s and recording techniques moved on with 12" vinyl records lasting 15 minutes each side and 7" LPs for home and juke-boxes in the new milk bars and cafes. Electrically operated radiograms with their superior sound quality were bought by the rich. They were made of veneered wood in a decorative shape, about the bulk of a washing machine, though slightly wider but slimmer, housing a radio, record deck and large speaker. Some decks could be loaded with several records. Then everything started shrinking. 1963 saw the introduction of high quality tape cassettes and their players, then CDs in 1982. Digital recording had arrived.

A radiogram

Revox, who made the ultimate in tape recorders, saw their business disappear overnight with the introduction of the electronic age. Now it seems the average child carries on its phone many thousand recordings of incredible clarity on a piece of plastic smaller than a postage stamp, or has it stored on his or her computer. Quality unimpared, crystal clear even if it has been played hundreds of times.

The amplification of sound has become a great art. Gone are the days of the megaphone, given way to electrically powered loud hailers. On recordings we can hear guitarist's fingers sliding down the string

The grooves on gramophone records got steadily excavated away by the passage of the needle. Gramophones had no volume control. The bell of my childhood fire engines has been replaced by a siren that forces a concentrated beam of sound in front of it which becomes immediately muted after it passes. In the 60s and 70s domestic speakers got larger and heavier; became pieces of furniture instead of items of equipment. That has now largely reversed with very small, high quality units like Bose.

Photography

The Nos. 1, 2, 2a and 3 "Brownie" Kodaks.

The No. 1 Brownie gives six 2¼ by 2¼ pictures, and the No. 2 Brownie six 3¼ by 2¼ pictures without reloading. The No. 2a Brownie gives 4¼ by 2½ pictures, and takes spools for either six or twelve exposures. The No. 3 Brownie gives pictures 4¼ by 3¼, and takes spools for either six or twelve exposures. The No. 2, No. 2a, and No 3 models have each a pair of finders, showing exactly the extent of view embraced by the film.

For the No. 1 Brownie, we supply a self-attaching finder at a small extra cost of 1/-

No. 1 .. **5/-**   No. 2 .. **10/-**   No. 2a .. **12/6**   No. 3 .. **17/6**

At about seventeen I became interested in photography. It was then quite expensive to get pictures developed and printed. Most people did not take vast amounts of photos. Probably one film a year, twelve photos. The ones they did take were usually printed in quite small sizes. but kept. Now people take endless photos on phones but how many will survive?

My aunt had a box Brownie and used it all her life while my father, prefered his little folding Kodak camera, but a pinhole in the bellows which were rather worn sometimes let in thin rays of light spoiling his pictures. He had his snaps developed at the shop. When I started taking photos I was an apprentice. To economise I bought the equipment to develop my own in a very small room that was once a toilet. Most of my surviving pictures from those years have discoloured as a result of insufficient washing after the chemical reaction of development.

My early memories of being taken to a professional photographer are of the man having a 10 x 8 inch plate camera on a tripod repeatedly diving under a large black sheet to check that we were in an artistic pose and in focus, an operation that seemed to take for ever. When I worked on the newspaper our photographer was still using a similar camera for all his work, because of the huge amount of detail stored on a large glass negative. I still have some of his boat prints for reference.

A folding pocket Kodak from the 1930's

167

Employment

There has been another major change. The 1950s were years of full employment. One left school expecting to find work and most of us found it locally. As a result families tended to stay in close contact, the children setting up home in the same neighbourhood as the parents and frequently also that of the grandparents. This allowed friendships started at school to continue into later career and business connections. A network of family and social associations that helped to ease life. There was a downside to this. Promotion was often only achieved when the person in the grade above died, or was promoted because of a death, or retirement, further up the ladder. In the 50s and 60s employers were reluctant to use personnel who had moved several times, regarding them as drifters, likely to move on and therefore unreliable, not worth training. Nowadays employers see these people as bringing a new outlook and skills for their company. Young people can often achieve rapid promotion, or indeed in some fields like sport, or the investment business, be regarded as too old, burnt out by their early forties.

Now it is often difficult to find work. Even students with good university grades sometimes end up in menial jobs. Many jobs are now passed over the internet to workers in countries with lower standards of living and consequently lower wages. Call centres for example and accountancy. Our steel, shipbuilding and car manufacturing facilities have largely disappeared and as a result the young must frequently move to far off towns for work. They meet their future husbands and wives from yet another part of the country, or from abroad, and are obliged set up home where they work. I believe it is totally immoral for any government, wishful of appearing to have reduced unemployment, to encourage thousands of young people to go to university and work hard for three or four years with the belief that it will provide a great future for them; the Government knowing full well that there will be insufficient jobs, and that many of the degree courses lead nowhere. These young folk are then left on the dole, discouraged, their aspirations shattered, only finding jobs offering incomes well below their expectations; plus the added burden of repaying their university expenses.

Certainly there is a need for very bright youngsters to go to university. The country benefits as well as the students, but they should be channelled into courses which are needed for the future of us all. Just how many sociologists and anthropologists do we need? I have met people with two doctorates in obscure fields now running restaurants because there is no demand for their skills. We are in danger of becoming a nation top heavy with chiefs and too few indians, meanwhile if one needs a qualified plumber, or electrician you may have a very long wait. The manual trades of the past are becoming increasingly high tech and can offer extremely high salaries, but need much of their learning to be done on the shop floor. A bricklayer apprentice can learn how to build a magnificent wall under cover at college, but only apprenticeship on the job will teach him how to cope three feet down a broken manhole in a narrow alley in the pouring rain.

Switzerland is a country that has tried to tackle this problem by working out what labour requirement will exist in various fields then only allowing around that number to be trained for them.

The Generation Gap

During the last fifty years there has been one enormous change in the social setup, brought about by 'The Pill'.

Prior to its invention all methods of contraception were risky, most young people married in their early twenties. There was increasing danger of pregnancy as the couple became more and more fond of each other and they succumbed to what is now regarded as a normal temptation. Living together prior to marriage was totally unacceptable unless they were far from home. If the girl was unfortunate enough to become pregnant the pressure to marry immediately to avoid a scandal was immense. I recall a sixteen-year-old boy living close to us being obliged to marry a girl of the same age in these circumstances. Prevention of a scandal was often seen as more important by parents than the suitability of the match. "You have made your bed and you must lie in it," was a frequent phrase of the time. Abortion was illegal and illegal abortions were extremely dangerous, frequently carried out by unskilled women, with death or the inability to conceive further children as a not infrequent outcome.

About 1966 several events happened in close order. Mary Quant introduced the miniskirt to the fashion world. Women's legs were suddenly on view as never before and almost in their entirety. Stockings, previously supported by suspender belts, now came with a slightly elasticated top and stayed up by themselves. Tights arrived in the UK very shortly afterwards. Underskirts, called petticoats, were discarded as impossible to wear with the mini and finally came "The Pill".

For the first time in human history women could control their destiny to the same extent as men. They took full advantage of it. So did the men. All of a sudden girls' knees were on view. A hand that ventured to casually touch a knee covered with a dress or jeans was suddenly on bare flesh. The old saying: "Be good, if you can't be good be careful and if you can't be careful remember the date" became history: or at least it should have done.

Now the reason to marry in haste had gone. Couples started to live together prior to marriage, to change partners, to postpone marriage for a few years and enjoy their new freedom without the worry of pregnancy. The consequence of this has been that many couples have continued this freedom, delaying marriage; waiting until they are well into their thirties, or later, before having their first child. I value the time spent with my grandparents. They had more time than my busy parents to play with me, to pass on family history, teach skills and just chat. They had quaint phrases from the previous century like "Don't vex me" or "Make haste" and could bring the past to life. They had the power to influence parents, mediate in disputes and to pass on wisdom born of long experience. With marriage delayed well into the thirties and the high proportion of second marriages later still, vast numbers of children will not enjoy that relationship. A sad loss to both children and grandparents who may never have the chance to meet one another. With many second marriages we are now moving from roughly four and sometimes five generations a century to only two-and-a-half or three.

Pollution and Smoking

In the past smog, a combination of smoke and fog has been the killer of thousands of elderly people and others with chest complaints. 1952 was particularly bad. In cities coal fires in houses, power stations, factories and steam trains sent up their chimneys clouds of black particles. In foggy weather this warm rising air quickly cooled and started to fall, much of the soot becoming trapped in the fog droplets. For example one dark, foggy evening in the 1960s, I was travelling from Battersea to Wimbledon, south London under normal city street lighting, I had the car window open so that, with my head out, I could see the white line in the centre of the road just below me. All traffic was moving at very slow speed, walking pace, or less. For a moment I lost sight of the worn white line and the dim red tail lights of the car in front, then my car stopped. I accelerated slightly but got no movement so I jumped out and felt my way to the front of the car to find my bumper was pressed firmly against a tree. There had been a right-hand bend in the road but I had continued straight on. The tree was quite invisible from the driver's seat. That and the huge number of respiratory deaths it caused was the reason for the banning of log and coal fires in many town areas and the introduction of smokeless fuels a few years later.

Cigarettes were sold in packets of ten or twenty, Wills Woodbines, a cheap brand also sold fives when I was a child, or shopkeepers would break a packet of ten. Cigarette cards included in each pack prior to the war failed to make a comeback, but the sale of tobacco products was enormous. Almost all adult men smoked, quite a lot of women also and we boys would get an older lad to go into the shop and buy a packet, its cost being shared between us. We would then hide in the bushes in the park and make ourselves feel sick by smoking them too quickly in case we got caught by an adult or worse, by the park keeper. I gave up after two goes, but affected a pipe when I was around eighteen or nineteen. Before I was twenty-one I accidentally sat on it, breaking the stem in half. On the way to the tobacconist for a replacement I suddenly thought: "This is daft, I don't really enjoy it", so turned round and went home. I may have smoked three or four cigarettes with friends shortly after that, but never since.

Smoke was completely unavoidable, in the cinema the fug from smokers interfered with the view of the screen. The beam of the projector cutting a pathway through the rising blue cloud. Cafes, pubs and clubs were smoke filled, their walls stained nicotine brown and always reeking of stale tobacco. Offices filled with ashtrays and were of a similar colour to the pub walls. Non smokers suffered. My first wife, a non smoker, died of throat cancer brought about by years of working as a journalist in an office of smokers all of whom subsequently died of lung cancer. A 100% wipeout. And one might say "Serve them right".

THE VIADUCT: In these Green days waste is sorted and, if possible, reused. Trains, now electric or diesel electric and cars are headed the same way. The tall chimney behind the railway embankment pictured overleaf is that of Ramsgate's long gone Dust Destructor. All waste except paper and metal ended up burnt in similar depots all over the country, the fumes were then belched back over the inhabitants to mix with the soot from industrial and domestic chimney fires and coal-fired steam trains. Note also the old signal bridge above the last carriage and the line of telegraph poles along the embankment. Only one conversation at a time could be transmitted down a wire. My picture is dated June 1957 and was painted over a number of mornings to get shadows in the right place.

172

There are always folk who will argue that their grandfather was a heavy smoking drunkard who practically lived in a workingmen's club and managed to reach a hundred and twenty. Fabulous, how many other people did he help down the road to a horrible death on the way. In 1962 the Government issued its first health warning that there was a direct link between smoking and cancer. It has only taken fifty years and countless more miseries and deaths to partly correct that disastrous situation. If you are a smoker take a walk round the cancer ward of your local hospital to see what is in store for you. Smoking drugs did not become a fashion until the mid 60s so is outside the scope of this book. We are still learning about their disastrous long term bad effects.

Divorce

Divorce was rare in the 30s and regarded as extremely shameful. There were 5,146 UK divorces in 1936. During the war years, 1939-1945, a lot of young couples were separated for as long as five years and their experiences during this troubled time changed them. Reunited at the end of the war they hardly recognised one another. Divorces in 1947 shot up to 60,000. The years of stress coupled with a "Live for today as we may well be dead tomorrow" situation had led to a relaxation of the previous moral order. I recall a young pilot and the daughter of one of the members of our chapel divorced, both immediately left the area to avoid the embarrassment that accompanied it. Divorcees would be requested to resign membership of clubs and associations. People would shun them in the street and they could become isolated in society. The general attitude of adults talking to young folk about sex outside marriage was to pretend it did not happen without disaster, while knowing it went on all the time. Young couples arriving at boarding houses and small hotels were often asked to produce their marriage license because the establishment wished to be seen as morally squeaky clean. By the 60s divorces in the UK had fallen by a third then rose through the 70s and 80s peaking in 1993 at 165,018. A lot of these by people who already had a divorce history. The current trend is about 40,000 lower in spite of the increased population.

Many children are now born to parents who are not married, or have no inten-tion to marry, while having a very stable, loving relationship. This is now regarded as normal, but children in a similar situation used to suffer abuse from others and be called bastards. Unmarried mothers were equally ostracised. These girls often moved away from their home area and the support, or total lack of support, of their family and created a story of their husband having died, or being away from home, in order to re-establish themselves as respectable citizens in the eyes of others.

Manston Aerodrome

Manston aerodrome on the outskirts of Ramsgate was one of the fighter stations closest to the French coast and scene of the many mad scrambles to get aircraft off the ground when enemy aircraft neared our shores. My father, a wartime fireman himself, told me how the airfield fire crews would rush to assist damaged planes often landing with very limited control due to either injured crew or major damage resulting in their undercarriage failing to work. He said the fire engine just drove at full speed towards the expected stopping point, if necessary straight through fences or hedges in an effort to evacuate the crew before the plane caught fire.

173

Aircraft guidance systems were far less sophisticated than nowadays and fog often meant a plane, damaged and already short of fuel, but unable to see the runway, having to fly many more miles in search of a landing place. Manston was one of the airfields fitted with "FIDO", an oil-fired flarepath that allowed aircraft to see the runway in foggy conditions. It could be turned on rapidly and extinguished immediately the planes had landed to hide them from any enemy aircraft in the area. Still in use when we returned to Ramsgate it provided a dramatic orange glow stretching far into the distance.

For a number of post-war years the base was used by the Americans for their Sabre jet fighters. Later, with the Cold War, the runway was extended to accommodate the huge six engined U2 spy planes that kept watch on Russia. The Americans were a mixed blessing to the locality, welcomed by local shopkeepers and of course by landlords who were able to charge profitable rents. They were less welcomed by the much poorer local lads who were severely handicapped financially. The American uniforms were very smart, of better quality than those worn by our own troops below the rank of officer, perhaps because of the shortage of cotton in Britain. Their USA pay scale was much higher and they were free spending which attracted the girls. Not only that, their base shop stocked goods unobtainable in the UK, unrationed food and nylon stockings which they gave to their girlfriends together with chewing gum for their brothers. "Got any gum chum" had become a catch phrase anywhere Americans were based.

They tried hard to join in with the local community and I am sure did much to help the post-war effort to return to a peacetime normality. There were also a number of unfortunate incidents. Napolion Green, a coloured American airman killed three men on the base and wounded seven others, highjacked a car to Broadstairs and on the beach, trapped by USA Military Police, finally shot himself. Several aircraft crashed and on at least two occasions swerved off the runway onto or across the public road, one decapitating a family in a passing car and another ending up embedded in a house. Of course there is nothing to prove that similar sad incidents would not have happened if the RAF had been based there.

Haircuts

This talk of airmen reminds me of National Service in the RAF and haircuts. Now styles have changed and changed back again and will do so for ever. Thank goodness the tools used to achieve the various effect have altered.

In my extreme youth there was a Mr Carden in King Street patronised fortnightly by my father who believed in discouraging the growth of his hair. Short and respectable was his attitude. You have to remember that in those days mixed sex hairdressers did not exist. Men went to barbers' shops, easily recognised as such by the white pole with a red spiral painted on it sticking out from their wall. The barber would give you a haircut or a shave and in days long gone would also do a bit of blood-letting if a person appeared to suffer from too high a colour. For me the single attraction of a visit to Mr Carden was the short ride in his dentist's type chair which was pumped up to a convenient height by a pedal. He had several pairs of scissors and several pairs of hand clippers such as are now in hairdressers' museums. *(See icon)* If you wished

THE BARBER'S SHOP

The barber's shop, until the late 1960s was a social centre for men only, a hive of information and a chance to read the paper while waiting for your turn. Discussions about politics or local affairs could get quite warm and as chairman the barber would frequently break from his work to keep order, after all he had to maintain good relations with both sides of a dispute. This inattention may have been the cause of my discomfort as he turned to them failing to complete a cut before tearing the clippers away from my neck.

to have hair long enough to be combed scissors were OK, but for the short areas like the sides or the back of the neck out came the clippers. I have to confess that his, to me elderly, customers were more stoic than myself, had suffered the Boer War in South Africa and the Great War and unemployment etc. Hard men, no fear, faces they had learnt to remain impassive even when screamed at by colour sergeant majors. I was of different material and as the roots of my hair were torn out by blunt clippers I grizzled, to the shame of my father and total indifference of the barber. During the war years we attended a hairdresser in the village used to caring for ladies hair and more attuned to my desire not to suffer. Back in Ramsgate after the conflict I was old enough to choose my own barber, but clippers still ruled though usually a little better managed.

Gradually, in the years following the Beatles era, unisex hairdressers have become the thing. Excellent, everything soft and namby pamby, cups of coffee, young ladies to wash your hair. A change for the better, much prettier than the barber, only one thing is missing. The conversation. Men used to chat to the barber. He knew everybody and was a source of information and the latest jokes. What can elderly men say to an eighteen- year-old girl hairdresser. Years ago we could have chatted them up....but now?

National Service

In the years following the war all young men in good health were required to serve in the Armed Forces when they reached eighteen years of age unless serving an apprenticeship, in which case they were deferred until it finished, usually at twenty-one. At its inception the period was two years, but relaxed to eighteen months as the demand for personnel decreased.

The end of WW2 did not result in world peace and our troops were involved in actions in Palastine from 1945-48 when the state of Israel was born. Also in Malaya 1948-60, Korea 1950-53, Africa against the Mau-Mau 1952-60, Cyprus 1955-59, Suez 1956, Malaya and Indonesia 1962-66 and Aden 1963-67.

I was deferred because of my apprenticeship and called up in September 1957 just after getting married. By then there was a policy of reducing strength. Prior to callup I was told to go to Chatham for a medical. This was conducted by a short, elderly doctor who hobbled in with the aid of a walking stick. By turn he held our testicles and asked us to cough, weighed us and measured our height. I was over six foot and he and was unable to reach the top of the measure, so poked it up with his stick and asked me to tell him the reading. The whole thing was a farce.

At the medical we had been allowed to express a preference for either Army, Navy or Airforce. This guaranteed nothing, but I was fortunate to get my choice and was duly issued with a travel warrant to Cardington in Bedfordshire with its enormous hanger, once the home of the R101 airship. The morning following my arrival we new boys were lined up for a much more thorough medical, blood test and injections. I never found out which as, at the medical, the Squadron Leader doctor said "I'm sorry lad, You have a polypus (like a wart) in your nose and no medical record of it. If you were posted to a hot country it could aggravate the situation and RAF could be obliged to pay you a pension. You are to be discharged". A year-and-a-half of my life given back to newly married me. I didn't know what to say. "Yipee" seemed appropriate, but then I thought perhaps this guy is spiteful and will say "Arr, but in your case I have decided now to make an exception." Alternatively, if I look sad he may be a kindly guy and say exactly the same thing. I remained absolutely poker-faced, said "Yes Sir" and left in haste. It took from ten o'clock in morning till four in the afternoon to get me signed into the RAF so that I could be discharged from it. I had served Queen and Country for twenty-six hours and during the following weeks was inundated with mail asking me to join the RAF Association, the Old Contemptables and the British Legion.

As a now fully fledged printer I had been paid £8.50p a week. As a National Service man I would have received thirty bob. *(£1.50p see p84)* Some men employed by their local authority continued to get their wages throughout their service career. Those in private industry got nothing but the meagre £1.50p. A considerable injustice. Employers were obliged to re-employ returning National Servicemen, but I decided to join a different company and was childishly pleased to tell the foreman of my original company that I would be working for the opposition at an improved rate of pay.

The changing business world

The following is an example of the way town centres have changed. Deprived of the old-fashioned shops where everyone knew each other, vast shopping centres developed on the outskirs of the town. As a young man my father had become managing director of a company with three branch offices supplying everything except flour to bakers thoughout Kent. My grandfather, the company secretary for almost fifty years had his stores and stabling for delivery horses attached to his town house which was conveniently close to a blacksmith when a horse needed quick reshoeing. By the end of WW2 he was well past retirement age and black-smiths were no longer needed, replaced by a garage. After weathering the war years the business soon suffered a new setback. As my grandfather put it: "We supply all the Kent bakers who pay their bills." However, shopping habits were changing. Men returning from around the world brought back with them a taste for alternative foods. To compete, shops needed more floor space and carried ever greater ranges of products. Many bakers had great difficulty paying bills.

Cinemas suffered a decline with the introduction of television in the early 1950s. The redundant theatres and vacant spaces in towns left by bomb damage were utilised to build larger, new style, self service stores. This was the beginning of the end for old style grocers, butchers and bakers. Factory produced sliced and wrapped bread was developed and sold through the newly created supermarkets started by Sainsburys in 1950, and soon joined by others. Private bakers started to close or go bankrupt. Soon there was insufficient room for ever larger stores, so trading estates were formed on the perimeters of towns, frequently destroying trade in the town centre which have in many cases been left with a few fast food shops, a chemist, fashion stores and charity shops.

Our bakery customers disappeared at the rate of one a week. For several years turnover fell and the directors stopped paying a dividend and drew no directors fees while working ever harder to reverse the situation. One of the advantages of a private company is that one can do this retrenchment instantly and without publicity. Public companies on the other hand must show a dividend, or see their share values crash, public confidence destroyed, and have great difficulty surviving a crisis. Luckily my brother, who had spent some time working for a food wholesaler prior to doing his National Service, now joined the company. He proposed a change of direction. Why not become food wholesalers to the newly booming hotel and boarding house trade. Due to his very considerable drive this proved a great success and turnover rose dramatically.

There was one further setback for us. The introduction of Cash and Carry ware-houses. A grocery chain with shops throughout much of Kent set up a large ware-house on the outskirts of Ramsgate to entice hotels and boarding house owners from delivered goods to cash and carry. This was in direct competition with us. For a time we lost valuable business to them but eventually they experienced stock control and reliable delivery problems. My brother finally negotiated a deal with them and we took over their hotel and boarding house trade together with two of their vehicles and some staff, though not their premises as we had by then also built a large new store near the outskirts of the town on a redundant dog racing track.

There are other alterations in the business world. Attitudes have changed as businesses became larger, then much larger. For instance the owner of a grocery shop had usually been brought up in the locality, knew his customers and their relationship within the community. He knew where he could allow credit, and who was likely to run into debt. So did the bank managers, usually local men known and trusted and able to make on the spot decisions about loans to their clients. The great conglomerates who now control food chains, chemists, hardware stores etc. make their decisions nationally. There is no consideration of individual needs either for staff or customers. It is all about maximisation of profit and minimising their taxation. The directors concern is to provide their shareholders with the best return on their investment. That is not wrong, but it is now lacking in the personal, friendly touch that was more prevalent in the past.

The other great change has been buying on credit. This was done in the past with sales from catalogues by tally men. Payments for goods were collected from buyers at their home each week and the tally man knew his customers and how much they could afford. It did him no good to over-sell as he knew he would have great difficulty recovering the debt and incur the anger of his employer. Modern hire puchase started after an Act of Parliament in 1957 and was tightened up in 1967 for the prevention of mis-selling. Unfortunately with credit cards, buy-on-line and easy acccess to credit many people have now been lured into enormous debt problems far beyond their ability to ever repay. The shortfall is made up by loading the price of products onto the rest of the population who have been more frugal with expenditure. They pay for the others irresponsibility.

Tools and Do-it-yourself

During my childhood all portable tools were hand operated. To be sure there were bench saws and planing machines powered by large DC electric motors in workshops but on site or in a boat yard, hand tools ruled. Augers and breast drills, hammers and chisels, tenon saws, bow saws, rip saws, smoothing planes, tryplanes, block planes, moulding planes, all hand operated and requiring a certain amount of experience and skill to do the job properly and to keep them adequately sharp. Large pieces of timber could be machined at the works, but much of the detailed fitting of cupboards and door frames etc. had to done on site as at present. It was not possible to go to the local Do-it-yourself store for the materials. The materials were held only by builders, and these for their own use; not for sale to the general public, consequently the builders were able to ensure that all building work was done by them, not the customer. I suppose that as it had always been the case nobody questioned it. After all nobody that I have heard of has knocked up a coffin for grandma, that is left to the undertaker. Why? Well nobody does it. Is that a reason? So these old ways of working go unchallenged for generations.

Perhaps it was the shortage of skilled folk to repair the vast ravages of bombing that fired the population to do their own work, or the cost, or the delays in getting new when a little time and patience could repair the old. Gradually the demand by people sparked off a new supply source independent of the builders. Today a huge industry has been built up selling everything necessary, pre-made. Ready to install furniture and fittings just needing a screwdriver and hammer, also a massive choice of materials if someone wishes to do the whole job to their own design.

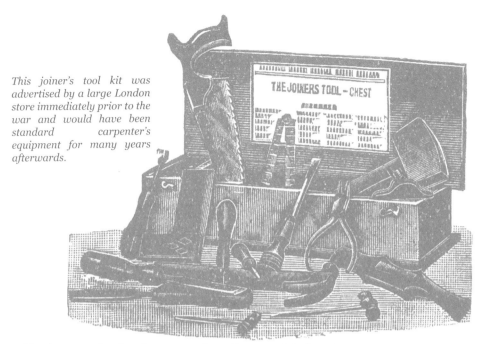

This joiner's tool kit was advertised by a large London store immediately prior to the war and would have been standard carpenter's equipment for many years afterwards.

The 60s saw the development of small, powerful electric motors, many now with rapidly rechargeable batteries, which has given birth to an enormous range of comparatively cheap, light, easy to use powered hand tools. Planes that trim a door to size in a few moments instead of half-an-hour of hard work. Tungsten tipped drills that make holes in concrete in seconds, diamond disc cutters that cruise through granite as if it was butter. Many householders have enhanced their homes at dramatically lower cost.

Materials for decorating and plastering have also been revolutionised. Fillers, glues and plaster finishes developed to make life easy for the less skilled. Wallpapers with plastic finishes that just need wetting for a few minutes in the bath before hanging. Earlier wallpapers needed more careful handling and if pasted for a different length of time strips could expand more than their neighbour so the pattern did not line up.

Oil paints used to contain lead and often required several days to dry between coats. Those of today dry fast and the water soluble plastic paints can often be used either inside or outside and be ready for recoating in a matter of hours. All these aids have given us much more warm, comfortable and elegant homes than those of our forebears. Draught free central heating beats an open fire at one side of the room every time, even in an Elizabethan cottage.

A wooden moulding plane.

Fast and foreign food

As rationing faded out and incomes improved the traditional British diet based on bacon and eggs, beef, lamb and pork was re-instated. Beef was king and chicken still a luxury. In the 1950s animals were still herded in, "on the hoof" as people used to say, from the surrounding countryside to be slaughtered in an abattoir near the town centre.

Fast food used to depend on the speed of the waitress and chef. British people did not eat strange foreign food. Of course Britain for countless generations had market stalls selling oysters, whelks and other shell fish etc., fish and chips wrapped in newspaper or eel and pie shops. Bakers supplied pies, pasties and ham rolls. These were the only shop type takeaway outlets. Lyons Corner Houses, a famous catering company, with different restaurants on each floor in major cities and one in all major towns were, so far as I can remember, the first outfit with Serve Yourself counters. In my Canterbury student days a very reasonable meal with a desert was about four shillings, (20p). While at art college I got ten shillings a week for lunches. Monday and Tuesday I pigged it, about three shillings a day. Wednesday was about two shillings, by Friday I was down to soup and a Chelsea bun. That's standard student life. Wimpey Bars followed Lyons example in 1954. A menu of tomato soup, roast chicken and trifle was voted people's top luxury meal in a 1949 Gallup poll. The mass breeding of broiler chicken did not start until the tail end of the 50s. Until then chicken was a comparatively expensive product.

Immigrants from the West Indies started to arrive in 1948 although their influence on food was negligible outside the cities. Prejudice against them was strong, England was white and anyway they had a different accent. There was a belief, even among educated people, that the coloured races were incapable of ruling themselves or of holding management positions. The terrible strife during the partition of Pakistan from India brought a flood of immigrants from both countries to Britain, many opened restaurants and introduced the choice of sit down or takeaway meals. Hot dog stalls then hamburgers came by 1962 when, at my father's suggestion, I spent a short while direct selling a brand of hot dog cookers for his business. My training was totally inadequate and we soon dropped the idea without noticeably damaging the hot dog market. Chinese restaurants also expanded across the country. I had my first Tandoori meal in Charlotte Street in central London, the city's first, in 1965/6 when Chicken Moglai was served with a sheet of pure silver leaf on top of it. I noticed this expense was rapidly cancelled when their later opposition failed to follow suite. By 1976 these had been joined by Greek and Thai restaurants. I first saw McDonalds in 1977 followed a little while later by pizzas. In recent years, Japanese sushi bars have joined the fray.

Drinking habits have also undergone a revolution. The British drank local brews in local pubs. Wine bars were non-existent. Our drinks were the likes of local draught brews, Guinness, stout and spirits. Wine was for those few who could afford holidays abroad. A teetotaller, brought up in a strict Methodist home to believe drinking alcohol a sin, I asked my father-in-law-to-be for an orange juice when invited to a Canterbury pub with him. He refused to get it, embarrassed to be in my company. In his view proper men drank, preferably in quantity and smoked sixty cigarettes a day. He and his wife died of lung cancer. The Methodists have now decided that an alcoholic drink is no longer the road to hell and damnation, a decision I reached many years before them having discovered wine when newly married in 1957.

Wine in bulk did not pour into the country until the 70s by which time holidays abroad were becoming popular, the unlikely front runners being Mateus Rose from Portugal together with Blue Nun and Black Tower from our recent enemy, Germany. The French were presumably still recovering from war or only selling at prices the mass market could not afford. By the 80s the UK was awash with wine, mostly from France, which has now lost out to the many other wine producing countries, who have modified their product to changing tastes and kept their prices affordable.

Keeping records

From ancient times all records were hand written. Large heavy ledgers recorded the purchases and sales of goods. Accounts were written by hand as were paid receipts which in my youth also had to carry a tu'penny stamp; this receipt tax was abolished in 1957 by act of Parliament. Births, marriages and deaths were inscribed with steel knibbed pens. Private letters were always hand written as it was

A pen and ink stand. The centre pot was for spare knibs.

considered rude not to take the trouble to write. Later, becoming more often used at home, the addressee's name and the signature of the sender were always put in by hand as a matter of politeness. Only business and Government letters were typed and even they were addressed and signed by hand or sometimes, in the case of Government, rubberstamped. If they contained an error they had to be entirely retyped until the introduction of Tippex in the early 60s. At work we used steel knibbed pens but many people had fountain pens. Ball point pens arrived in 1945. From Victorian times to the 40's and 50's office desks bore two inkwells, one for blue and the other red, each with its own pen, a ruler and a blotter as ink dried slowly and was easily smudged. Adding machines for pounds, shillings and pence were, like typewriters, totally mechanical and often almost as large as typewriters. *(See icon above.)* A Mr Goldsmith in our office could add up the three columns of cash simultaneously in his head faster than anyone else using the machine. He

A Royal office typewriter.

was a strange character and frequently wrote to King George VI, the Prime Minister and the Archbishop of Canterbury offering his advice, or explaining where they had gone wrong. They were awfully polite and sent him letters no doubt via a junior secretary thanking him for his trouble. He would then bring the letters to the office to show everyone.

In the advertising world prototype advertisements were frequently required with minor alternatives or in duplicate, and needed complete redrawing for each variation. That was until the introduction of photocopiers in the early Fifties. Unless a typewriter carbon copy was good enough, documents required in duplicate had to be written twice. Photocopiers together with Letraset, a method of transferring preprinted letters onto a layout, caused enormous unemployment in the advertising industry and many of my art school colleagues finished their graphics course in the mid 50s to find there were no jobs available. Electric typewriters were gaining popularity in the early 60s. These had much more sensitive keyboards and had carbon ribbon instead of fabric giving a much sharper impression. The keyboards of the older machines had to be struck quite firmly especially as the ink ribbon got old, or letters wore out, or got damaged due to several letters being mis-struck at the same time. *(See the Ministry letter on pages 48-49.)*

Through the 70s computers gradually gained ground though with very limited power compared with those of today. They required a special room with purified air to avoid any dust contamination or temperature change and they were large. At first input to them was by punched cards. Our family business entered the computer age in 1979 with an IBM machine costing £53,958, superseded after only four years by one much more powerful costing considerably less, in turn replaced by PCs at ever lower prices and of vastly increased capacity. I read recently that today's mobile phone has far more computing power than that used to control the rocket for man's first moon landing.

Finally

This book was not intended to be a definitive study of all the progress made between the mid-Thirties and the mid-Sixties. It is an account only of how some of the many changes have affected the lives of much of the population including my own. I hope it has recalled memories to those of my own generation and painted a picture of some of their experiences for those of you who arrived much later.

There have been countless other modernisations and inventions during that period and huge changes in the fifty years since then. Our language has changed along with everything else and continues to do so. "Cool" described the temperature in the cellar; a happy carefree person was described as "gay" and a "mouse" was the unfortunate creature my mother pulled from a trap when my memories began. My generation of British natives have had extraordinary good fortune. Born too late to suffer the depression years, too young to take part in the war although, as National service men we may have experienced war in other countries. We have not been called to defend our homeland. We have been the first generation to enjoy medical care regardless of income, beneficiaries of financial support if out of work or disabled and some sort of supporting pension in old age. We have seen our children grow up with the possibility of further education at college or university and women freed from the drudgery of washing. Our houses are almost all centrally heated; we can expect several weeks paid holiday each year and are able to choose from a vast selection of affordable destinations. We expect to live longer than our forebears and to be healthy enough to benefit from the extra years. There are endless organisations available to amuse us as we dodder through our declining time and if we feel so inclined we can write books about "Life when I was your age" to bore the pants off our children. I can only hope that succeeding generations will be as fortunate as we have been.

THE END

... but please turn to the next pages for enlarged icons and the Reference Index ...

*The following selection of
icons has been enlarged for
the benefit of those with
less than perfect sight and
also those who enjoy
looking at pictures.*

13 Police helmet 1930's

15 Lettered phone dial

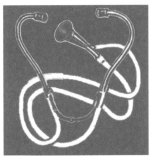
17 Stethoscope

18 Monday washing

19 Smiling sandwiches

20 Triplane

22 Civilian gas mask

30 Land mines

31 Air raid equipment

33 Scrap metal

34 Polka dot ladies

35 Ice cream

185

37 Church affairs

39 Grocer's shop

44 Coal and coke scuttle

50 Broken eggs

52 Scything

58 Bombed out boarders

62 Make do and mend

66 Stook of wheat

73 Hops

81 Girl's games

84 Shop till

88 Measurements

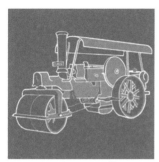

89 *Steamroller*

94 *Bad manners*

96 *Apple picking*

99 *Sweet rationing*

100 *Mr Littlehaler's shop*

103 *DDay gliders*

105 *Doodlebug*

109 *Wallpaper corner*

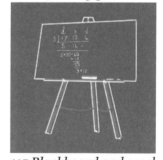

115 *Blackboard and easel*

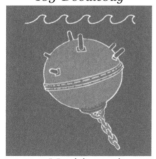

119 *Maritime mine*

120 *Housing situation*

124 *Queuing for food*

126 Camp fires

130 Seaside holidays

132 Manual labour

139 Charladies

143 The Harbour

149 Platen printing press

151 Spare time

158 Austin Ruby 1937

162 A Teddy boy

166 Gramophone

169 Four generations

172 Pollution

174 Hair clippers

177 Bedford van 1937

180 Fast food

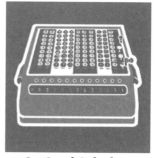

181 £:s:d Calculator

Pulling one and a half tons like one horse but faster and nobody needed to get up at 6am to feed it, clean out the stable and groom it, or bed it down at night.

As a teenager I could ask for "cod and six of chips" (meaning six pence worth of chips.) Total cost 2s 6p. (Twelve and a half pence) Plaice was only 1s 9d. (a little under 9p) A really good meal.

Like the old Royal type-writer, this machine was entirely mechanical.

Reference Index